解析柏拉图
《会饮篇》

AN ANALYSIS OF PLATO'S SYMPOSIUM

Richard Ellis　Simon Ravenscroft ◎ 著
李梦千 ◎ 译

目 录

引 言 ……………………………………………… 1
    柏拉图其人 2
    《会饮篇》的主要内容 3
    《会饮篇》的学术价值 4

第一部分：学术渊源 ……………………………… 7
    1. 作者生平与历史背景 8
    2. 学术背景 13
    3. 主导命题 18
    4. 作者贡献 22

第二部分：学术思想 ……………………………… 27
    5. 思想主脉 28
    6. 思想支脉 32
    7. 历史成就 37
    8. 著作地位 42

第三部分：学术影响 ……………………………… 47
    9. 最初反响 48
    10. 后续争议 53
    11. 当代印迹 59
    12. 未来展望 63

术语表 …………………………………………… 68
人名表 …………………………………………… 72

CONTENTS

WAYS IN TO THE TEXT	81
Who Was Plato?	82
What Does *Symposium* Say?	83
Why Does *Symposium* Matter?	85
SECTION 1: INFLUENCES	87
Module 1: The Author and the Historical Context	88
Module 2: Academic Context	94
Module 3: The Problem	99
Module 4: The Author's Contribution	103
SECTION 2: IDEAS	109
Module 5: Main Ideas	110
Module 6: Secondary Ideas	115
Module 7: Achievement	120
Module 8: Place in the Author's Work	126
SECTION 3: IMPACT	131
Module 9: The First Responses	132
Module 10: The Evolving Debate	137
Module 11: Impact and Influence Today	143
Module 12: Where Next?	148
Glossary of Terms	153
People Mentioned in the Text	158
Works Cited	164

引言

要 点

- 柏拉图是公元前 5 世纪至 4 世纪的古希腊哲学家,西方"哲学之父"之一。
- 《会饮篇》用一场虚构的对话来阐明爱欲与德性的关系。
- 该著作不论在文学样式还是在哲学思想上都具有革新意义;两千多年来,一直影响着人们对于爱情、欲望和德性的思考。

柏拉图其人

古希腊哲学家柏拉图是苏格拉底*的门徒,是各哲学传统中最著名、影响最大的哲学家之一。我们虽然难以考证他准确的生卒年份,但通常认为他大约生活在公元前 425 年至公元前 348 年之间。他在古希腊的雅典城邦工作,并在那里建立了名为"柏拉图学园"*的哲学学校,它被认为是西方世界同类学术机构中的第一所。柏拉图进行写作与教学的时期正处古典时期,雅典是当时的知识和文化中心——一个哲学辩论与知识交流的核心区域。

算上一些真实性存疑的篇目,柏拉图的哲学对话录现存 30 余篇,包括《会饮篇》和一些被称为"书简"的书信。这些对话录采用哲学辩论的形式,辩论发生在当时的一些人物之间,包括哲学家苏格拉底。他们讨论诸多问题,涉及德性生活和智慧的构成(伦理问题)、国家及其理想的统治形式(政治问题)、人类学识的特性和对真理的追求(认识论*问题),以及现实世界的基本结构(形而上学*问题)。

柏拉图的思想在其去世后仍然在"柏拉图学园"和雅典的其他哲学学校被讨论,随后在古代地中海文明和其他文明中流传。柏拉图被称为"西方哲学之父",他与他的学生亚里士多德*一起奠定了绝大多数西方哲学流派的基础。柏拉图的思想以各种方式渗透于西方的精神文化中,也影响了其他文明的思想家,比如中世纪的伊斯兰哲学家阿尔-法拉比*。柏拉图思想的重大影响持续至今。

《会饮篇》的主要内容

《会饮篇》的形式为虚构的对话,对话发生在当时雅典著名的演说家、思想家和作家之间,他们谈论着关于爱与德性的问题。文本以在"会饮"上发生的一系列对话为主要结构。会饮是一种晚宴,在宴会中,上层阶级的男人们可以得到物质享受、身体快感(通过食物、酒饮和性)以及一些更加高雅的精神娱乐(通过学术探讨)。每一段讲话都"赞颂爱欲*"——"爱欲"是一个古希腊术语,指与性欲有关的爱的形式,也是现代英语形容词"色情的"的词根。

《会饮篇》所探讨的基本问题是爱欲在对智慧、德性与幸福的哲学追求中所起的作用。具体说来,它探讨爱欲是否有助于哲学的产生以及合乎道德的生活。虽然文本采取了开放式的对话形式,没有发言者得出明确的结论(这意味着对话可以有多种解释),但我们完全可以认为,柏拉图以一种积极的方式展示了爱欲与哲学和德性生活之间的联系。柏拉图借老师苏格拉底之口尤为清晰地阐明了这一点。

对诸如人类身体等美的物质的爱欲可以催生(如柏拉图笔下的苏格拉底所说的)对更加高尚和文雅之美的欲望和爱,如知识、德性和智慧的美。的确,爱欲最终还是引导我们对美本身的凝视——哲学的终极目的。文章中描述的这一过程被称为"美的提升"*,对这一过程的论述是西方哲学传统中最著名的篇章之一。最终,爱欲被认为对个人的幸福和安宁与社会整体的利益都起着至关重要的作用。

《会饮篇》被视作柏拉图最具影响力的作品之一，它在两个方面对后来的作家和思想家都产生了深刻的影响，这并不令人感到意外。

其一是其文学的独创性。柏拉图构想出一场晚宴，在这场晚宴上，哲学的辩论以一种轻松甚至喜剧的方式进行。通过这一构想，柏拉图创造出一种哲学式的文学，且后世不乏效仿者。[1]

其二是它对爱和爱欲及其同德性和伦理的关系的讨论，这几乎形塑了后来所有对于这一问题有重要性的讨论。例如，柏拉图的学生亚里士多德，在他的《尼各马可伦理学》中对爱欲的关注则较少。即使是在今天，柏拉图和亚里士多德作品中的分歧仍在引发许多围绕爱之"理想"形式的讨论。

最后，从一个更加广泛的意义来说，鉴于柏拉图的思想对西方思想界尤其是对哲学的普遍影响，《会饮篇》作为柏拉图庞大的作品体系（他的文集）的一部分，具有重要的学术和文化意义。

《会饮篇》的学术价值

《会饮篇》引导我们去了解柏拉图这位思想史上最具影响力的哲学家之一。单就这一点来说，其内涵就值得我们深思。

人们普遍认同柏拉图的假定，即要回答怎样才能将生活过得最好这个问题，对《会饮篇》的核心主题——爱、欲望、德性、智慧和幸福——进行思考是必不可少的。古代哲学与现代学术性的哲学不同的是，它明确和不断地关注"好的生活"这一问题。的确，在许多方面古代哲学本身就被理解为一种实践和生活方式，[2]

在《会饮篇》中这一点体现得很明显。这个文本探讨欲望——特别是爱欲——如何有助于德性之道与对智慧之追求。甚至在今天,《会饮篇》还在引导我们去反思,我们可能拥有什么样的人生?特别是当我们碰到同欲望和爱有关的问题时,我们会如何去思考,去行动。

这部作品的形式也很值得注意。《会饮篇》的结构很复杂,它的长篇"谈论"并没有明确地解释其观点。对于它所提出的问题,也没有给读者提供一个简单的答案。对于现代学术性的写作来说,如此明显地缺乏清晰性会被视作败笔。然而,在柏拉图的作品中,清晰性的缺乏可以让我们明白,对智慧和真理的追求并非一蹴而就;对于人生中的问题,我们也不可能总能找到简单明了的解决方案。

《会饮篇》让我们明白,学术研究不仅是一个寻找答案和学习事实的过程,还是一个发展有益的思考与交流方式的过程,即柏拉图所谓的理智德性。即使是对非哲学专业的学生来说,这也是有价值的一课。

最后,从更普遍的意义来说,柏拉图特别是《会饮篇》,对西方思想和文化的影响是如此的深远,以至于研究这部作品就等于理解现代文化所继承的文化传统。

---

1. 理查德·亨特:《柏拉图的〈会饮篇〉》,牛津:牛津大学出版社,2004年,第9—10页,第126页。
2. 皮埃尔·阿多:《哲学作为生活的一种方式:从苏格拉底到福柯的精神实践》,迈克尔·查斯译,牛津:威利-布莱克威尔出版社,1995年,第49—70页,第147—178页。

第一部分：学术渊源

1 作者生平与历史背景

要点

- 《会饮篇》催生了一种新的哲学式文学,自其写成之日起一直影响着有关道德、爱和欲望等主题的讨论。
- 柏拉图是苏格拉底的学生与追随者,而苏格拉底在《会饮篇》中是关键人物之一。
- 会饮是古希腊的一种社交活动;在宴会上,人们可以享受美食、美酒和性所带来的身体快感以及思想上的精神愉悦。

为何要读这部著作?

柏拉图的哲学对西方思想有着巨大的影响,《会饮篇》在这方面发挥了重要作用。作为柏拉图作品体系(他的文集)中的核心作品,《会饮篇》也是柏拉图最另类、最有挑战性、最晦涩难懂的作品之一。

作品虚构了一场柏拉图与同时代几个人物之间的对话。这场对话发生在"会饮"(一种晚宴)上,且没有得出一个确切的结论。这也许是一种有些复杂的文学形式,但它在风格上具有高度的创新性,并且催生了一种全新的哲学式的文学类别。[1]

作品的核心主题是爱欲对追求美德与哲学真理可能起到的促进作用。柏拉图虚构了人物的对话,他对这一主题的反思就体现在这些讲话中,这极大地影响了西方思想界。受影响者众多,从他同时代的古典时期哲学家,如他的学生亚里士多德,到一些最重要的基督教*的神学家(指研究上帝的人)如圣奥古斯丁*。这种影响直到现代仍然在各领域学者的作品中有所体现。许多世纪以来，由于其文学的独创性、哲学价值以及跨越世纪的文化影响，《会饮篇》与讨论相关主题的《吕西斯篇》和《斐德罗篇》一道，一直是人们乐于研究的课题。

> 无论是在会饮上进行的对话，还是通常在此类活动中发生的情色关系，都是探索（古希腊文化中）欲望伦理的自然方式，因为语境本身就试图使爱欲朝着某种文化规范的方向发展。
>
> —— 弗里斯比·C.C.谢菲尔德：《柏拉图的〈会饮篇〉：欲望伦理》

作者生平

通常认为柏拉图于公元前 425 年出生在雅典附近，家世显赫。他的父亲阿里斯顿可追溯至雅典以前的某一任国王，他的母亲珀克里提俄涅则出自梭伦*家族，梭伦是公元前 6 世纪晚期雅典著名的立法者之一。[2] 柏拉图在雅典长大，这是一个思想家、诗人和哲学家云集的城市。他接受过雅典上流阶级典型的精英教育。在参加如绘画、诗学特别是悲剧等创造性的活动之前，柏拉图在私人学校学习了文法（正式的学术与文学作品）和摔跤。[3]

在青年时期，柏拉图常常和哲学家进行谈话与辩论。据记载，柏拉图受到一位年长的思想家的影响，这位思想家熟识赫拉克利特*的观点，认为世界的本质和结构是通过动态的发展变化来维持的。[4] 后来，柏拉图遇见了哲学家苏格拉底，很快便成为了他的追随者。苏格拉底对柏拉图的人生与哲学思想影响最大，他也是《会饮篇》中的关键人物。

与大多数雅典人一样，柏拉图拥有多神信仰*。这意味着他相信有多位神或者女神的存在。宗教仪式是政治生活和社会生活的一部分，这使得很多现代研究者觉得，很难将古代雅典人的宗教身份与公民身份*完全区分开。特别值得注意的是，柏拉图同一些神秘宗教的接触。在这些宗教里，政治和宗教的身份是一体的，因为上天的启示只对被挑选入会的那部分人披露。举例来说，发生在雅典附近的厄琉息斯秘仪*就为《会饮篇》中上升至"美的理念"*的仪式提供了背景。[5] 在该作品的描述中，哲学家在进步，从渴望物质的事物如美丽的肉体到渴望非物质的事物如精彩的观点，最后达到对美本身的凝视；美在永恒不变的形式中，超越物质与时间。

创作背景

柏拉图很有可能在古希腊世界的思想中心——雅典创作了《会饮篇》。雅典被誉为"卓越的开明城市"[6]，是一个极具商业性、制度性、诗性和哲学性的地方。在那里，思想在剧院、法庭、公共集会和哲学辩论中产生并传播给热切的听众。在雅典建立了他的哲学学校柏拉图学园之后，柏拉图一直在这片培育了他的肥沃的学术土壤上耕耘。

柏拉图《会饮篇》的标题呼应了它所虚构出来的背景：一个仅有男性的社交场合，可以饮酒、进餐、交流学识以及进行一些其他形式的娱乐活动，通常包括音乐和性方面的有偿活动。在古希腊世界，会饮是上流男性的社交活动。它代表的不仅是一次晚宴，更是一个文化价值和理念得以在一代又一代人之间产生和传播的场所。[7] 事实上，它还是一个贵族的"另类社会"[8]，与之并行的是公元前5世纪的雅典城邦，一个更加民主、开放的社会体系。因此，这个标题不仅呼应了柏拉图这一哲学论著*的背景，也体现了作品的知识文化框架。

虽然《会饮篇》在公元前约380年写成，[9]但其所描写的那场虚构的晚宴却发生在公元前416年（也就是30年前）。其"阵容"包括那个时期几位最重要的人物——哲学家苏格拉底、剧作家阿里斯托芬*和阿伽颂*，以及臭名远扬的年轻将军阿尔西比亚德斯*。在公元前416年之后，这位将军对雅典和斯巴达*之间的伯罗奔尼撒战争*的结局起了关键作用。[10]

在公元前380年的读者眼中，《会饮篇》不仅思考关于德性与欲望的永恒的哲学问题。它借历史人物之口来表达这种思考，这些人物对于当时的人们来说本身就具有重要意义。更加值得一提的是，这种语境是在公元前399年由《会饮篇》的主角之一苏格拉底提供的。苏格拉底影响了雅典人的想象，他也是柏拉图生命中最重要的人物。《会饮篇》所描述的他的生动形象，一定会让人们隐隐想到他被定的罪：使雅典的青年堕落，对城邦的神不敬。[11]

---

1. 理查德·亨特：《柏拉图的〈会饮篇〉》，牛津：牛津大学出版社，2004年，第9—10和126页。
2. W.K.C.格思里：《古希腊哲学史·柏拉图其人和他的对话：早期》（第4卷），剑桥：剑桥大学出版社，1986年，第10页。
3. 格思里：《古希腊哲学史》（第4卷），第12—17页。
4. 格思里：《古希腊哲学史》（第4卷），第33页；黛布拉·奈尔斯：《柏拉图那些人：柏拉图和其他苏格拉底派的群体传记》，印第安纳波利斯：哈克特出版社，2002年，第105—106页。

5. 弗里斯比·C. C. 谢菲尔德:《柏拉图的〈会饮篇〉:欲望伦理》,牛津:牛津大学出版社,2006年,第219页。
6. 史蒂文·伯格:《情欲与启蒙的沉醉:论柏拉图的〈会饮篇〉》,纽约州奥尔巴尼:纽约州立大学出版社,2010年,第x页。
7. 亨特:《柏拉图的〈会饮篇〉》,第5—7页。
8. 亨特:《柏拉图的〈会饮篇〉》,第6页。
9. K. 多弗,"柏拉图〈会饮篇〉的日期",《明智》1965年第10期,第2—20页;亨特:《柏拉图的〈会饮篇〉》,第3页。
10. 亨特:《柏拉图的〈会饮篇〉》,第4—5页。
11. 伯格:《情欲与启蒙的沉醉》,第x—xii页。

2 学术背景

要点

- 古希腊哲学关注事实的本质和美好人生的特性等基本问题。
- 在《会饮篇》的那个时代,通常认为爱欲(即爱和性欲望的影响)与哲学对"美好人生"的追求之间并没有本质的联系。
- 柏拉图将爱欲作为哲学和德性生活的基础来进行颂扬,以此质疑当时的一些普通看法。

著作语境

古希腊语中,哲学这个词的本意为"爱智慧",由希腊语单词"philia"和"sophos"组成。进行哲学学习的人,主要专注于现实的基本结构和德性生活的本质问题。如毕达哥拉斯学派*,他们将世界理解为一个紧密结合的数学体系。据说,柏拉图在意大利南部与毕达哥拉斯学派的哲学家有过一段时间的接触。[1]

柏拉图也受到更早期的哲学家如巴门尼德*和赫拉克利特的影响。巴门尼德的理论认为,我们的感官机能使我们难以认识到存在的统一、不变和永恒的本质。[2] 该理论暗含了对赫拉克利特的批判,他认为宇宙处于一种持续不断的变化状态中。[3] 然而,对柏拉图产生最大直接影响的人是苏格拉底。

对柏拉图那个时代的雅典公民来说,"德性的本质"是一个很值得探讨的话题,不论是在会饮或是其他场合中。[4] 爱欲的概念是需要调节的含混的*(模棱两可的)外部力量。[5] 在剧场里悲剧的描绘中,爱欲能够让人违背自己的意愿去行动;当公民大会被政治家的言论动摇时，它还被用来形容公民大会的非理性行为。[6]

> 不论是在形式还是内容上……《会饮篇》都与柏拉图对美好生活本质的更大的伦理关怀密切相关。那种所有谈话者都关心的情色关系常常发生在会饮上，并且被视作品德传授的重要方式。
>
> —— 弗里斯比·C.C.谢菲尔德：《柏拉图的〈会饮篇〉：欲望伦理》

学科概览

值得思考的是柏拉图对于智者*的看法。智者属于知识阶层，他们有偿地教授修辞学*（如何有效地说话与辩论）和论辩*艺术（争吵与辩论）。柏拉图在《普罗泰戈拉篇》中说智者认为自己能够传授德性，他们对听众来说是很有吸引力的。但当时社会上的一些保守派对智者表示反对。柏拉图也在作品中对他们进行了严厉的批判，说他们只对金钱和享乐主义*（追求享受）感兴趣，因此可能会损害易受影响的学生的灵魂。

对于柏拉图来说，哲学既是一种教育形式，也是一种生活实践。他认为哲学应该是免费传授的，这本身也是哲学的主要目标之一，而智者显然不具备这一品德。[7] 柏拉图对智者所教授的修辞形式对教育的破坏性影响深感不安。在思考他有关爱欲在哲学中的运用的探讨时，也应该考虑到他的这种焦虑感。

还应该注意到的是古希腊文学传统对柏拉图思想的影响。古希腊道德观念主要由荷马*史诗*塑造，而在公元前5世纪的雅典，喜剧和悲剧的剧作家非常活跃，他们也深刻、具体地影响了柏拉图的思想。的确，《会饮篇》中塑造的人物本身就有剧作家，改编了戏剧中探索过的主题、形象和思想（尤其是爱欲的不可抗拒的力量和效果）。在古希腊文学中，爱欲常常被视为一种不可抗拒的外部力量，它使人们违背良好的判断和建议。[8] 柏拉图对于爱欲的较为积极的刻画，也应该考虑到这些方面。

学术渊源

据亚里士多德所说，柏拉图的第一次哲学经历来自赫拉克利特学派的克拉底鲁，柏拉图年轻时曾与他有过交往。[9] 在柏拉图吸收赫拉克利特的一些思想时，他拒绝接受赫拉克利特的核心理论，即一切都处于一种不断变化的状态中，或者更确切地说，整体的稳定性只能通过持续的变化来实现。不同的是，柏拉图的形而上学给出了一种更重要和完美的世界形式，它是不变的，这与赫拉克利特的可感知的变化世界形成对比，而柏拉图的理解才道出了获得真正的知识与德性的关键。[10]

毫无疑问，对柏拉图影响最大、最直接的还是他的老师苏格拉底，柏拉图在《会饮篇》中把他放在了核心的位置。然而，研究者们很难将苏格拉底自己的观点与柏拉图赋予他的观点区分开[11]，因为我们并没有苏格拉底看法的第一手资料。明确一件事对另一件事所产生影响就是所谓的"苏格拉底式问题"的根源。这个问题长期以来都被认为是"无法解决"的。[12]

通过回应当时就爱欲与哲学关系的争论，《会饮篇》从根本上改变了辩论的状况。通过作品中苏格拉底的那段最长的发言，柏拉图重申了爱欲作为一种内在的动力促进着哲学反思与德性追求。[13]柏拉图以这种方式质疑了主流观点，该观点认为爱欲是一种具有侵入性的力量，会引发非理性行为。

柏拉图通过描述一场虚构的会饮达到了他的目的。虽然它本身并不是一次破天荒的文学尝试，但却是第一部为了对道德和欲望进行哲学探讨而描述会饮的作品。因此，我们可以说，这部作品的精髓在于文学之形式与哲学之内容的结合。

《会饮篇》并不是凭空出现的，而是基于文化中的文学、哲学和社会因素而成。柏拉图的创新之处在于，他以对话的形式使陌生的观点和派别之间相互交流，从而创造了全新的著作。

---

1. W.K.C.格思里：《古希腊哲学史·柏拉图其人和他的对话：早期》，剑桥：剑桥大学出版社，1986年，第35—36页。
2. 格思里：《古希腊哲学史》（第4卷），第34—35页。
3. 格思里：《古希腊哲学史》（第4卷），第33页。
4. 弗里斯比·C.C.谢菲尔德：《柏拉图的〈会饮篇〉：欲望伦理》，牛津：牛津大学出版社，2006年，第4—5页。
5. 谢菲尔德：《柏拉图的〈会饮篇〉》，第5页。
6. 理查德·亨特：《柏拉图的〈会饮篇〉》，牛津：牛津大学出版社，2004年，第16—18页。
7. 玛丽娜·麦考伊：《柏拉图论哲学家与智者的修辞》，剑桥：剑桥大学出版社，2011年，第1—3页。
8. 亨特：《柏拉图的〈会饮篇〉》，第17页。
9. 黛布拉·奈尔斯，《柏拉图那些人：柏拉图和其他苏格拉底派的群体传记》，印第安纳波利斯：哈克特出版社，2002年，第105—106页。
10. 格思里：《古希腊哲学史》（第4卷），第33页。
11. 威廉·普赖尔："苏格拉底（历史学的）"，选自《柏拉图指南》，杰拉尔德A.普雷斯编，伦敦：绵延出版社，2012年，第29—30页。

12. 普赖尔:"苏格拉底(历史学的)",第29页。
13. 柏拉图:《会饮篇》,选自《柏拉图:〈会饮篇〉》,M.C. 豪瓦斯顿译,M.C. 豪瓦斯顿与弗里斯比·C.C. 谢菲尔德编,剑桥:剑桥大学出版社,2008年,第32—50页。

3 主导命题

要点

- 《会饮篇》旨在回答两个关键问题:爱欲的本质是什么?爱欲与真理和德性的哲学追求之间有什么关系?
- 爱欲通常被认为是一种具有侵略性的、不可知的外部力量,常常违背理性。
- 与一般观点不同,柏拉图认为,爱欲**可以**为追求德性与智慧以及真正理解美提供一个良好的基础。

核心问题

柏拉图《会饮篇》通篇的核心问题,就是爱欲究竟是不是有助于对哲学的追求。柏拉图的答案是肯定的,并且认为爱欲不论是对个人的品德还是集体的凝聚力都非常重要。为了理解柏拉图在《会饮篇》中赋予爱欲的重要性,我们有必要了解他对于当时文化环境的独特理解。

作品中的探讨发生于一场虚构的会饮上——雅典上层阶级男性的、具有文化意义的社交场所。[1] 古代会饮的一个重点是它是进行少年爱行为的场合,它是不同年龄的男子之间的约定。一般说来,较为年轻的与会者会获得较为年长的对其德性和知识方面的指导。[2]

当然,在这些关系中,核心是对另一个人的身体的爱欲。虽然对这些活动都进行了很细致的审查,并且常常受到指控称其会使人堕落,但《会饮篇》还是探讨这样的(性)关系如何能够说明、促进甚至充当各类德性与智慧的基础。这一点在柏拉图借苏格拉底之口发表的长篇讲话中体现得尤为明显。

> 由于（在传统上）爱欲是一种侵入式的外力，它可能让人感到羞愧和迷失方向，因为它使人丧失正确的判断力和独立意识；爱欲迫使我们面对我们的不足和欲求，这便是《会饮篇》的基本观点。
> ——理查德·亨特：《柏拉图的〈会饮篇〉》

参与者

在以前的古希腊文学中，爱欲被描述为一个很重要的生命原理，它使得不能永生的生物得以繁衍延续，也让大自然得以丰产。据说，爱欲的感觉类似于雨水对于大地的渴望。[3]

大致上，"从最广泛的意义来说，在古典时期诗歌中，爱欲被视作一种入侵力量或情感，它驱使人们渴望得到感官上的满足。"[4] 这种"侵入式的强力"常常被描述为一种难以名状的力量，这种力量充斥着主体，并且让人为了追求欲望而失去理智。由于这种力量常被视为神的行为，爱欲同样也被看作一种神的力量。例如，在欧里庇得斯*的戏剧《美狄亚》和《希波吕托斯》中，美狄亚和菲德拉都经历过这种无法控制的强力。[5] 它使人对其渴望的事物感到莫大的缺乏感，又使其充满一种想要填满这种匮乏的难以抵挡的冲动。这样一种对于爱欲的理解构成了柏拉图在《会饮篇》中所讨论的主题的思想和文化背景。

当代论战

与当时的主流观点不同,柏拉图认为爱欲并不是一种无法控制的外部影响,而可能产生于内心,并且可能有利于德性的获得与保持。

虽然柏拉图反对主流观点,尤其是在他笔下苏格拉底的言论中,[6] 但他并没有与那些对爱欲的解释持相反观点的作家和思想家们进行正面交锋。作为一部产生于具有广阔思想潮流背景的古雅典的作品,《会饮篇》对于爱欲的阐释本身就足够出色了。而且,正面交锋也并不适合柏拉图为其作品所选择的文学形式,即多个谈话者之间的对话。

柏拉图让每一位发言者以爱欲为主题作一篇颂词(即一种赞美性的讲话)来相互竞争。柏拉图将艺术模仿与抽象的哲学论证融合在一起,模糊了严肃论著与戏剧的界限,从各个方面对爱欲进行积极的描绘。柏拉图将爱欲与匮乏联系起来(特别是在阿里斯托芬的言论中,他将爱欲定义为"对整体的欲望和追求"),[7] 强调了一种对于他同时代的人来说已经很熟悉的观点。与此类似,在《会饮篇》中,柏拉图借阿尔西比亚德斯之口表达了"爱欲表示缺乏理性"的观点。阿尔西比亚德斯的口中,哲学就像有毒的爱欲咬伤"心脏或灵魂"而造成的"迷狂和狂热"。[8]

作品的复调*特性——即包含多个观点——及其转述的叙述手法让人很难对其所论证的哲学主题进行准确的界定。不过,人们一般将第六段讲话,即苏格拉底的讲话视为《会饮篇》的核心观点,因为这一观点与柏拉图其他作品有所重合。

1. 理查德·亨特:《柏拉图的〈会饮篇〉》,牛津:牛津大学出版社,2004年,第5—7页。
2. 亨特:《柏拉图的〈会饮篇〉》,第5—7页;弗里斯比·C.C.谢菲尔德:"导读",《柏拉图:〈会饮篇〉》,M.C.豪瓦斯顿译,M.C.豪瓦斯顿与弗里斯比·C.C.谢菲尔德编,剑桥:剑桥大学出版社,2008年,第viii—x页。
3. 亨特:《柏拉图的〈会饮篇〉》,第17页。
4. 亨特:《柏拉图的〈会饮篇〉》,第16页。
5. 亨特:《柏拉图的〈会饮篇〉》,第17—18页。
6. 柏拉图:《会饮篇》,选自《柏拉图:〈会饮篇〉》,M.C.豪瓦斯顿译,M.C.豪瓦斯顿与弗里斯比·C.C.谢菲尔德编,剑桥:剑桥大学出版社,2008年,第32—50页。
7. 柏拉图:《〈会饮篇〉》,第26页。
8. 柏拉图:《〈会饮篇〉》,第57页。

4 作者贡献

要点 🔑

- 爱欲能让哲学家看到美的理念本身,即纯正德性的来源。
- 《会饮篇》讨论了爱欲对德性生活和美的本质的积极贡献,观点具有开创性。通过撰写《会饮篇》,柏拉图创造出了一种新的哲学式的文学类型。
- 在古希腊,会饮是集性爱、教育、知识的传授和道德论争与对话等活动于一身的社交场所。柏拉图利用这些活动来达到他的哲学目的。

作者目标

在《会饮篇》中,柏拉图的主要目的是讨论爱欲与伦理、幸福、真理和教育之间的关系。这样一来,他对于道德、伦理和爱欲的哲学探讨与他同时代的人并不相同。柏拉图通过精心构造的文学作品来做到这一点,他将自己的观点非常巧妙地嵌入一段叙述中(例如,在《会饮篇》中指发生在会饮上的一场虚构的对话)。

公元前约6世纪,会饮通常是诗人们用来进行道德思考的场所,如麦加拉的泰奥格尼斯*和米蒂利尼的阿尔凯奥斯*。历史学家希罗多德*(公元前5世纪)在一本关于地中海区域历史与民族的著作中有过相关的描述。[1] 然而,是柏拉图以他的论述、哲学思想的深刻性以及对于智慧人士间知识活动的描绘,开创了将会饮视作学术性晚宴的传统。在这种宴会上,哲学是一种娱乐的方式。[2]

会饮上七位发言者的讲话体现了作品的主题。柏拉图之所以构建这样一场虚拟的对话,旨在使对话能够得到丰富和补充、批判与修改,使对话的主题和观点得以重新强调或削弱。

苏格拉底是第六个发言者,他的讲话最长也最富有哲理,被认为体现了作品的核心主题,回答了其他发言者的问题。³ 柏拉图在此处提出了革新性的观点:若"正确地"对待欲望,爱欲就能够为对德性和智慧的哲学追求提供积极和丰厚的根基。

> 一个人想要循着正确的途径去接近……爱,应该从这个世界上美好的事物开始,并且将这些事物当做阶梯,为了追寻其他的美而向上攀登,从一个到两个,再从两个到一切的形体,更从美的形体到那些美的行动,从美的行动到美的知识,最后从各种美的知识达到那种完全关于美本身的知识,于是人终于认识了真正的美。
>
> —— 柏拉图:《会饮篇》中苏格拉底的讲话

研究方法

《会饮篇》中的七位发言者每人都作了一篇颂扬爱欲的讲话。对于从整体上理解作品,每一篇讲话都很重要,但对于柏拉图的核心问题来说,最令人惊奇的还是他在作品中赋予苏格拉底的讲话。其观点极具新意,即认为对美的爱欲能够促进对德性与智慧的哲学追求。

这一观点在有关"美的提升"的著名论述中是最为详尽的。根据这个观点,人们由爱欲驱动着,从对美好形体的体验达到对美的灵魂的爱,并且由此再到对法律、制度以及知识体系之美的欣赏。最后一步就是看见并理解美的理念本身,即某种处于不断变换的表象世界之外的东西。⁴

柏拉图笔下苏格拉底讲话的核心观点就是，当以一种正确的方式和秩序去实现对美好事物的爱欲时，它将有利于德性与智慧的获得。在这个意义上，爱欲应该被视作理性与哲学的积极因素，而不是一个障碍。

虽然柏拉图想将苏格拉底的发言设计为一段意义深刻的讲话，但整部作品的文学结构让我们不能仅仅根据苏格拉底的话语就得出一个确切的结论。的确，在他讲完话后，整部《会饮篇》的基调都变了，那个喧闹的政治家阿尔西比亚德斯与一伙会饮常客闯入了宴会，他近乎醉酒状态下对于苏格拉底本人的赞扬改变了谈话的氛围。[5] 柏拉图利用阿尔西比亚德斯的言论，强调了解读苏格拉底以及发掘其言辞中真理与智慧的难度。[6] 这个发言告诉我们："不论是阅读这部还是其他柏拉图的作品都需要付出努力和思考，都要求我们真正地'进入'到苏格拉底的言词中。"[7] 柏拉图在《会饮篇》中通过这种方式将文学与哲学结合在一起，既新颖，又对读者有吸引力。

时代贡献

与当时的普遍观点相反，柏拉图认为爱欲能够作为一种内在的力量促进德性的兴盛。

会饮提供了一个场合，在这个场合里，情色活动与教育、教学活动一同发生。[8] 柏拉图将他的哲学探索嵌入一场对话中，并置于这样一个场景下，是极具创新性的。

虽然他采用了在当时不同寻常的文学形式，但他依然借鉴了一些较早期哲学家的思想。例如，《会饮篇》对于爱欲的作用及其重要性的探讨，就借鉴了公元前 5 世纪中期哲学家恩培多克勒*的观点，这一借鉴在柏拉图赋予阿里斯托芬与厄里什马克*的发言中体现得最为明显。[9] 恩培多克勒认为宇宙的自然进化和变化由争斗和爱的竞争力量驱动——虽然他使用的是古希腊词语"友爱"（爱或友情），而不是柏拉图所使用的更强烈的"爱欲"（爱或欲望的力量）。柏拉图对爱欲进行探索，将恩培多克勒的宇宙力量转化为一种内部力量，其能将个人与其爱人结合在一起，同时又提供了获得无止境德性的可能。

在柏拉图赋予苏格拉底的话语中，美被形容为抽象且永恒不变的。苏格拉底认为，对美的凝视能够产生真正的智慧。这个观点源自爱利亚的巴门尼德。巴门尼德是公元前5世纪早期的哲学家，他认为可感知的世界（即我们能够通过感官察觉到的世界）是一个虚幻的假象，掩盖了真实的、不变的、永恒的、形态为完美球体的事实存在。柏拉图的理念论* 及理念在获得知识的过程中所起的作用，在一定程度上借鉴了这个理论。通过对《会饮篇》的阅读，我们认识到哲学实践让我们超越物质世界达到抽象的美的境界。柏拉图不同于巴门尼德的地方在于，他认为，我们需要接受教育以瞥见"美的理念"，而在这样的教育中，爱欲扮演着重要的角色。

---

1. 理查德·亨特：《柏拉图的〈会饮篇〉》，牛津：牛津大学出版社，2004年，第14—15页。
2. 亨特：《柏拉图的〈会饮篇〉》，第9—10和126页。
3. 柏拉图：《会饮篇》，选自《柏拉图：〈会饮篇〉》，M.C. 豪瓦斯顿译，M.C. 豪瓦斯顿与弗里斯比·C.C. 谢菲尔德编，剑桥：剑桥大学出版社，2008年，第32—50页。
4. 柏拉图：《会饮篇》，第48—49页。

5. 柏拉图:《会饮篇》,第 51—63 页。
6. 柏拉图:《会饮篇》,第 55—57 页。
7. 亨特:《柏拉图的〈会饮篇〉》,第 11 页。
8. 亨特:《柏拉图的〈会饮篇〉》,第 5—7 页;弗里斯比·C. C. 谢菲尔德:"导读",《柏拉图:〈会饮篇〉》,M.C. 豪瓦斯顿译,M.C. 豪瓦斯顿与弗里斯比·C. C. 谢菲尔德编,剑桥:剑桥大学出版社,2008 年,第 viii—x 页。
9. 凯瑟琳·H. 朱克特:《柏拉图的哲学家:对话的连贯性》,芝加哥:芝加哥大学出版社,2009 年,第 289—290 页。

第二部分：学术思想

5 思想主脉

要 点

- 《会饮篇》探究爱欲的本质及其与哲学和伦理生活的关系。
- 以正确的方式和秩序来追求爱欲能够产生德性与智慧。
- 该作品由发生在特定社交场合的一系列对话组成,每一段赞扬爱欲的讲话都与其他讲话相互印证。

核心主题

在《会饮篇》中,我们看到的是一场虚构的争论,争论的主题是情欲之爱——爱欲的本质及其与智慧和伦理生活之间的关系。

会饮的每一位参与者都被要求"作一篇礼赞爱的讲话",[1] 他们从神话、文学、医学、历史和哲学领域寻求灵感来提出对于爱欲的不同定义。通过这篇对话,作品探讨了有关伦理、社会和教育的主题:如何传授智慧;如何培养尊重与勇敢的意识;如何保持身体、情感和精神的健康;灵感和卓越是如何产生的;一个人如何通过对美的凝视来实现智慧、真理与幸福。

最重要的一段讲话,即柏拉图借苏格拉底之口发表的言论,试图解释,如果爱欲这种欲望被合理地对待,它如何为对真理和德性的哲学追求奠定一个基础。

《会饮篇》借这些观点的表达方式(在社交活动上的一系列对话)强调了如男性之间友情本质等的问题,也对如修辞对于真理之影响的问题提出一些见解,这一问题贯穿柏拉图的很多作品。[2]

> 一个人如果一直在学习爱的过程中受到指引,并以正确的方式和秩序凝视各种美的东西,那么在学习的最后阶段他将突然发现一种无比奇妙的美,即美本身……他为了看见美本身付出了先前的全部辛劳。
>
> —— 柏拉图:《会饮篇》中苏格拉底的讲话

思想探究

柏拉图的主要观点最清晰地体现在他借苏格拉底之口所说的话中。

苏格拉底认为,先前的发言赞美的是发言者本身而不是爱欲的本质。[3] 他说,那些发言所赞扬的是被爱者的品质,而不是那使人去爱的爱欲本身。苏格拉底认为爱欲是对至美的难以控制的追求;并且,最美的东西也一定是最好的:"事实上,人们唯一爱的事物,就是好的事物。"[4]

但是,这种追寻并不以对"美好"的占有而结束。它旨在产生"智慧和其他的德性……城邦和家族的良好秩序……温和与公正。"[5] 换句话说,爱欲作为一种对美的和好的事物的追求,它本身也作为一种实践与哲学生活紧密地联系在一起,而这种实践的目标就是德性。

苏格拉底探析最精彩的段落就是著名的对"美的提升"的论述。[6] 在这部分中,一个追寻德性与真理的人,是首先由对物质世界之美的欣赏,如人的肉体,而逐渐上升至对非物质事物的欣赏,如灵魂之美以及知识的理式。其终极的目标,是看见并且理解那个恒久不变的"美的理念"本身。每一件值得凝视的事物都有一定的美,而那个"美的理念"本身就是永恒且不变的:"它不出现也不消失……它存在于它自身，它在本质上是单一且恒久的。"[7] 当爱欲得到谨慎的宣泄时（据苏格拉底说），它就能够带领我们达到那个境界。

语言表述

《会饮篇》的主题体现在柏拉图所描述的那场会饮上的七段发言中。作品的结构使得那些对爱欲的本质及功能的描述能够彼此印证与充实。因此，我们有必要思考作品的哲学观点及其得以呈现的方式。

柏拉图似乎意识到了这一点。他在他的作品体系里称，他那个时代的修辞实践更关注说服和吸引读者，而不是真理。苏格拉底的发言可以说是自我指涉的，他以指责之前的谈话者开始，认为他们更像是在赞美自己而不是爱欲，讽刺道："好像每个人只需要做做样子，并不需要真正地颂扬爱欲。"[8] 如果修辞学的目的是说服（如柏拉图似乎承认的那样），它不会自动地让一个"成功"的论点成为真理，并且，它同时也与论点提出者意图的纯粹性无关。

值得注意的是，《会饮篇》并没有就知识的探求得出一个确切的结论。作品没有在苏格拉底完成他的讲话时结束，而是结束于在场的人都睡着了的时候。[9]

我们也许难以对文本进行准确的解读，但这并不是文本的缺点。对于柏拉图来说，最重要的目的是鼓励读者继续追求智慧，质疑前人的判断，并且对于任何被称为知识之物的基础进行重新评估。从这种意义上来说，《会饮篇》没有为读者提供需要铭记的、封闭性的教条，而是一系列有利于哲学实践的质疑与观点。

柏拉图有关"美的提升"的篇章被认为是西方哲学和文学中最

令人印象深刻的论述；确实，人们认为它"在很大程度上塑造了欧洲的想象力"。[10] 它同时也精巧地概括了柏拉图对于哲学活动的目的及其在教育中的作用的观点。

虽然就柏拉图的整体思想而言，《会饮篇》的终极意义仍然有待解读，但它真正地转变了"哲学"这个学科，也就是说，将对智慧的"友爱"转变为对智慧的"爱欲"，即对爱与个人永续的渴望。

---

1. 柏拉图：《会饮篇》，选自《柏拉图：〈会饮篇〉》，M.C. 豪瓦斯顿译，M.C. 豪瓦斯顿与弗里斯比·C.C. 谢菲尔德编，剑桥：剑桥大学出版社，2008年，第7页。
2. 玛丽娜·麦考伊：《柏拉图论哲学家与智者的修辞》，剑桥：剑桥大学出版社，2011年，第1—3页。
3. 柏拉图：《会饮篇》，第33页。
4. 柏拉图：《会饮篇》，第43页。
5. 柏拉图：《会饮篇》，第47页。
6. 柏拉图：《会饮篇》，第48—49页。
7. 柏拉图：《会饮篇》，第49页。
8. 柏拉图：《会饮篇》，第32—33页。
9. 柏拉图：《会饮篇》，第63页。
10. 格雷戈里·弗拉斯托斯："柏拉图以个人为爱的对象"，选自《柏拉图主义研究》，格雷戈里·弗拉斯托斯编，新泽西州普林斯顿：普林斯顿大学出版社，1973年，第24页。

6 思想支脉

要点

- 阿里斯托芬的发言讲述了一个由初始的缺乏所致的爱欲的原始神话。
- 通常认为阿里斯托芬的发言提出了一种关于性别与两性关系的原始理论,它的要点与苏格拉底发言的核心论点有所不同。
- 厄里什马克发言的哲学价值常常被人们忽略。

其他思想

在柏拉图的《会饮篇》中,所有发言的主题都有关爱欲(欲望的力量,通常与性爱相联系)及其与友情、道德、教育的关系。虽然对这一主题的讨论最为精彩的部分要属柏拉图的老师苏格拉底的发言,但剧作家阿里斯托芬和政治家阿尔西比亚德斯的观点也同样很值得我们注意。阿里斯托芬和阿尔西比亚德斯在表达观点时,生动地谈及戏剧性的神话,有力地描述了爱欲那既使人脆弱又治愈人的力量。

阿里斯托芬的发言讲述了一则柏拉图独有的神话,它有关人类这个种族的起源,其中,爱欲来源于一种非常古老的缺乏。[1] 柏拉图将总结性的发言安排给了阿尔西比亚德斯,他同时探讨了爱欲的身体维度及其同哲学"迷狂"之间的关系。

> 所以我们每个人都只是一个人的其中一半,一条去骨鱼的其中一边,一种合起来才能完整的东西。所以每个人都一直在寻求自己的另一半。
>
> —— 柏拉图:《会饮篇》中阿里斯托芬的发言

思想探究

　　阿里斯托芬关于人类种族起源的神话是柏拉图特有的，也是他最具新奇性的想法之一。[2] 他在讲话中声称，目前人类这种并非永生的状况是一种退化的状态；也就是说，我们人类从前是一种圆球形并且有着两幅面孔的生物（分为三个性别：男－女、女－女或男－男），宙斯为了惩罚我们，将人类一剖为二。于是，现在与另一半分开的我们，不得不去寻求另一半来使自身得以完整。（据柏拉图笔下的阿里斯托芬所说）正是这种原始的配对决定了我们爱欲的对象。

　　因此，爱欲被描述为一个治愈者，它能够使凡人回到幸福和完整的状态，他的作用就是"通过二元性的统一治好人类这一毛病，还原到自己原来的整体。"[3] 换句话说，欲望有其自身的起源，这种起源就是原始的缺乏；并且，当一个人不去解决这种缺乏时，他就会处于一种消沉与倦怠的状态中。这种观点与古希腊有关性别分类以及性别范畴的主流观点背道而驰。[4]

　　对于爱欲的这样一种描绘与《会饮篇》中其他人的观点截然不同，它较少地关注爱欲同教育与德性间的关系问题。它提出了一种让人惊奇的研究爱欲的视角，并且它所提出的有关情感满足的质疑一直吸引着后世的读者。[5]

　　同苏格拉底的发言一样，阿尔西比亚德斯的发言也讨论了爱欲对于真正德性的形成以及在哲学家"美的提升"过程中所起的作用。在《会饮篇》的结尾部分，他的发言将读者从苏格拉底那抽象的理智主义拉回到了个人身体与情感的欲求上。[6] 阿尔西比亚德斯将哲学描述为一种"迷狂与狂热"，它是爱神对"心脏或灵魂"的毒咬导致的。⁷ 这种观点不同于苏格拉底对于爱欲之"美的提升"的更为和谐的论述，并且与当时的主流观点更为一致，即认为爱欲是一种侵入性的、动摇人心的力量。

当被这样咬了一口之后，阿尔西比亚德斯说："在这世上就没有什么［一个人］不会去说、不会去做的了。"⁸ 阿尔西比亚德斯是一个历史人物——一个被暗杀了的具有争议的政治家与军事家，柏拉图选择借这样一个人物来表达这种观点，这一决定本身就留下了关于哲学、爱欲和政治生活（该作品的潜在主题之一）之间复杂联系的问题。⁹ 他的发言也强调了《会饮篇》呈现给读者理解上的困难。他将苏格拉底及其话语比作西勒诺斯*神雕像，这些雕像里面还有着更小、更美丽的雕像。"我不知道还有谁看见过他内部的那些神像，但是我看到过一次，它们对我来说是如此的神圣、金光闪闪而又无比的美好奇妙。"¹⁰

这既是一种告诫，让我们不要轻易相信表面现象，又是一种象征，象征着可能被掩盖了的德性的真正伟大。对于理解苏格拉底和其他发言者的讲话，这一点非常重要。¹¹

被忽视之处

根据传统的解读，我们应该将阿尔西比亚德斯、阿里斯托芬和苏格拉底的发言视作柏拉图最重要的形而上学观点（形而上学是指对现实的基本结构的研究）。然而医生厄里什马克的发言常常被人们忽视，人们通常认为它的言论"更加难以理解"或者说"仅认为其拙劣地模仿了公元前5世纪那充满行话的科学与医学的'宏大统一理论'"。¹²

厄里什马克试图以"美好"与"恶劣"的两种爱来解释艺术与

科学的统一，依次采用多种学科来解释他的观点。[13]"为了尊重我自己从事的行业，我愿意先从医学出发"，[14]他的话语常常被认为是过于自我甚至自私的。[15]（这可能尤其体现在他运用赫拉克利特哲学时自视甚高的态度）。[16]厄里什马克对于细枝末节的过度关注，使得一些读者认为柏拉图倾向于讽刺一种思想类型而不是细致地去探寻一种理念。因此，这段发言被评判为几乎没有哲学价值。然而，厄里什马克没有像一开始看起来那样严肃地对待自己的观点，但这个观点已经渐渐让人们认识到他的发言是如何对《会饮篇》起到积极作用的。这个课题还有很大的研究空间。[17]

1. 柏拉图：《会饮篇》，选自《柏拉图：〈会饮篇〉》，M.C. 豪瓦斯顿译，M.C. 豪瓦斯顿与弗里斯比·C.C. 谢菲尔德编，剑桥：剑桥大学出版社，2008年，第22—27页。
2. 柏拉图：《会饮篇》，第22—27页。
3. 柏拉图：《会饮篇》，第24页。
4. 杰弗里·卡恩斯："不是一个神话：柏拉图〈会饮篇〉的话语建构"选自《重新思考性：福柯与古典时期》，大卫·H.J. 拉莫尔等编，新泽西州普林斯顿：普林斯顿大学出版社，1998年，第105页。
5. 理查德·亨特：《柏拉图的〈会饮篇〉》，牛津：牛津大学出版社，2004年，第68—69页。
6. 柏拉图：《会饮篇》，第51—63页。
7. 柏拉图：《会饮篇》，第57页。
8. 柏拉图：《会饮篇》，第22—27页。
9. 参见史蒂文·伯格：《情欲与启蒙的沉醉：论柏拉图的〈会饮篇〉》，纽约州奥尔巴尼：纽约州立大学出版社，2010年，第x—xii和131—150页。

10. 柏拉图:《会饮篇》,第 56 页。
11. 黛博拉·塔恩·斯泰纳:《思维里的图像:古希腊古老和经典文学与思想中的雕像》,新泽西州普林斯顿:普林斯顿大学出版社,2002 年,第 89 页。
12. 亨特:《柏拉图的〈会饮篇〉》,第 54 页。
13. 柏拉图:《会饮篇》,第 18—22 页。
14. 柏拉图:《会饮篇》,第 18 页。
15. 凯文·科里根和埃琳娜·格拉佐夫-科里根:《柏拉图的辩证法:〈会饮篇〉的论点、结构与神话》,宾夕法尼亚州大学公园:宾州州立大学出版社,2004 年。第 63 页。
16. 柏拉图:《会饮篇》,第 18 页;科里根和格拉佐夫-科里根:《柏拉图的辩证法》,第 63—65 页。
17. 亨特:《柏拉图的〈会饮篇〉》,第 53—59 页。

7 历史成就

要点

- 柏拉图在《会饮篇》中对爱、欲望、美和德性的探索，从古典时期*（中世纪之前）至今一直对西方思想有巨大影响。
- 作品不论在文学形式还是在哲学观点上都具有创新性，这使其重要性持续至今。
- 基督教对作品的神秘主义的*解读，一度掩盖了作品对于身体性欲的强调。

观点评价

《会饮篇》的整体氛围虽然幽默，但其旨在描述一场严肃的哲学活动，因此它被认为属于"亦庄亦谐*"的文学类型，即古希腊的悲喜剧。[1]《会饮篇》作为一部悲喜剧，对整个西方的思想文化都产生了历史影响；毫无疑问，柏拉图非常成功地实现了他的目标。他将诗学、修辞学与哲学融合进一个精心建构的虚拟场合中，给读者制造挑战，让其在这样一个或被比作晚宴的场合中进行哲学思辨。

《会饮篇》诙谐幽默的文学特点是其核心要素之一，它成为后来悲喜剧作品的典范。[2] 柏拉图的目标是寓教于乐，为了实现这个目标，在讨论欲望和爱欲同伦理之间的关系以及对智慧与德性的追求时，他从根本上改变了这场讨论。

几千年来，《会饮篇》在各类不同的语境中被改编与引用，其所留下的文化遗产是如此的纷繁复杂。然而，我们可以确定的是，柏拉图被公认为整个西方哲学传统的思想之父。[3]《会饮篇》不是一部可以直截了当地解读的作品，它的七段有关爱欲的谈话持续为后来的哲学家、理论家及其他领域的学者提供灵感与启发。

> 《会饮篇》一直以来都是柏拉图被阅读得最多、最有影响力并且被模仿得最多的作品。毫无疑问，这与其主题的广泛吸引力有关……但也因为作品本身的丰富多样，再加上读者并不需要太多的哲学训练就能阅读它，这些都使得《会饮篇》在受众接受柏拉图思想的方面享有盛誉。
> ——理查德·亨特：《柏拉图的〈会饮篇〉》

当时的成就

想要重建《会饮篇》当初的接受语境已经不可能了。两千多年已经过去，没有什么物质材料可以帮助我们。然而，我们大概可以推测出，该作品最先的读者应该就是柏拉图在雅典所建的哲学学校——柏拉图学园里的学生们。柏拉图学园的建立间接表明当时雅典的思想文化是非常丰富的，而这一定为该作品的成功贡献良多，同时它也为柏拉图的哲学论辩提供了自然的接受土壤。

哲学话语（或者说更加宽泛的"对话"）的价值使得柏拉图成为一位思想家和教师。在《会饮篇》中，他生动地描写了古希腊雅典著名人物，比如哲学家苏格拉底、军事将领阿尔西比亚德斯和喜剧作家阿里斯托芬，借鉴当时的政治、哲学和文学史为这一话语作出贡献。这些对于他最初的一批读者来说具有很大的吸引力。

柏拉图的学生（尤其是亚里士多德）以及其他对《会饮篇》作出回应的人，如伊壁鸠鲁（公元前4世纪末期的哲学家，伊壁鸠鲁*

学派的创始人）承担起了保护其文化遗产的责任。伊壁鸠鲁认为世界是由机会统治的，简单的快乐也应该得到高度的重视。伊壁鸠鲁和亚里士多德都撰写了他们自己的宴饮会话来回应柏拉图的《会饮篇》——虽然没有具体的细节留存至今。[4]

后来，古典时期的其他哲学家如斐洛*和普鲁塔克*仿照柏拉图的原作来撰写这种宴饮会话。这些作品都批判性地探讨了《会饮篇》中的道德和伦理立场，并且沿用了《会饮篇》的写作风格，在轻松的场合中探讨严肃的哲学思想。[5] 亚里士多德在他的《尼各马可伦理学》中也（间接地）回应了柏拉图关于爱欲与德性的理论。[6]

柏拉图学园的学生如普鲁塔克在柏拉图去世后的很长一段时间都还在对《会饮篇》进行探讨。普鲁塔克特别关注柏拉图将爱欲描绘为一个神灵（在神与凡人间进行沟通调解的中介精灵）来探索神灵在弥合神与凡间之鸿沟的作用。[7]

普鲁塔克在自己的作品《伊西斯与奥西里斯》[8]中，也借鉴了《会饮篇》来捍卫希腊和埃及的一种宇宙论观点（宇宙论是关于宇宙起源和发展的科学），该观点将化身为神的爱欲与埃及的神荷鲁斯*以相结合，这是一种宗教性的整合，用术语表示为"综摄"*。

局限性

虽然柏拉图的《会饮篇》反映的是公元前 4 世纪早期雅典的伦理、哲学以及文化问题，但其文学性与哲学性让它产生了广泛的吸引力。然而，从历史角度来看，它的某些观点比其余的观点更为突出。毕竟，不同的年代有着不同的重点、偏见及关注点。

在这种情况下，我们应当注意到文本在基督教时代的思想语境中是如何被接受的,尤其是在普罗提诺*和希波的奥古斯丁关注到该文本之后。普罗提诺是公元3世纪的哲学家,[9] 希波的奥古斯丁是一位基督教思想家,他根据基督教语境对《会饮篇》的改编是最具影响力的改编本之一。人们通常认为《会饮篇》中苏格拉底谈到的"美的提升"是希波的奥古斯丁爱的神学之基础,[10] 它描述基督信徒的提升和进步,就像站在梯子上向着神圣之爱攀爬。

许多年之后,15世纪的基督教哲学家马尔西利奥·费奇诺*对《会饮篇》进行了基督教的重新解读,他删除了作品中强调男性身体的性吸引力的相关内容。[11] 这些内容更偏向生理层面的性欲和爱,如果说对其的压制是基督教对柏拉图《会饮篇》典型的神秘主义解读,那么近来的性别理论者们又重新强调了这种解读。[12] 从这个角度上说,《会饮篇》的核心思想一直塑造着西方思想界对于爱、欲望与伦理问题多样化的思考方式。

---

1. 理查德·亨特:《柏拉图的〈会饮篇〉》,牛津:牛津大学出版社,2004年,第9页。
2. 亨特:《柏拉图的〈会饮篇〉》,第9—10和126页。
3. A.N. 怀特海:《过程与实在:宇宙论研究》(修订版),纽约:自由出版社,1978年,第39页。
4. 亨特:《柏拉图的〈会饮篇〉》,第14—15页。
5. 亨特:《柏拉图的〈会饮篇〉》,第121—123和125页。
6. 亚里士多德:《尼各马可伦理学》,戴维·罗斯译,牛津:牛津大学出版社,1980年,第196—201页;理查德·克劳特:"导论",《亚里士多德〈尼各马可伦理学〉布莱克威尔指南》,理查德·克劳特编,牛津:布莱克威尔出版社,

2006年，第9页；A. W. 普莱斯：《柏拉图和亚里士多德的爱与友谊》，牛津：牛津大学出版社，1989年，第85—86页。

7. 罗伯特·艾斯纳：《多利斯之路：精神分析，心理学和古典神话》，纽约州锡拉丘兹：锡拉丘兹大学出版社，1987年，第220和222—223页；米歇尔 A. 卢切希："普鲁塔克爱的理论与政治实践"，选自《古希腊的爱欲》，埃德·桑德斯等编，牛津：牛津大学出版社，2013年，第217—218页。
8. 亨特：《柏拉图的〈会饮篇〉》，第131—132页。
9. 普罗提诺："爱"，选自《九章集》，斯蒂芬·麦克纳译，伦敦：企鹅出版社，1991年，第174—186页；亨特：《柏拉图的〈会饮篇〉》，第130—131页。
10. 伯纳德 V. 布拉迪：《基督之爱》，华盛顿特区：乔治敦大学出版社，2003年，第79页。
11. 马尔西利奥·费奇诺：《论柏拉图式的爱——柏拉图〈会饮〉义疏》，西尔斯·杰恩译，得克萨斯州达拉斯：春季出版社，1985年；亨特：《柏拉图的〈会饮篇〉》，第134页。
12. 见大卫·霍尔朴林："柏拉图与情欲叙事"，选自《古典的革新》，丹尼尔·塞尔登和拉尔夫·赫克斯特编，纽约州纽约：劳德里奇出版社，1992年，第95—126页；夏伦·贝尔："圣妓之墓：《会饮篇》"，选自《精神的暗影：后现代主义与宗教》，菲利普·贝里和安德鲁·韦尼克编，伦敦：劳德里奇出版社，1992年，第198—210页；杰弗里·卡恩斯："不是一个神话：柏拉图〈会饮篇〉的话语建构"选自《重新思考性：福柯与古典时期》，大卫·H.J.拉莫尔等编，新泽西州普林斯顿：普林斯顿大学出版社，1998年，第104—121页。

8 著作地位

要点

- 柏拉图在作品中展现了一个全面的，或者说碎片化的哲学视野，其所涉及的主题也很宽泛。
- 通常认为《会饮篇》是柏拉图中期的作品，在主题上与《吕西斯篇》《斐德若篇》相关，也与柏拉图更广泛的伦理关怀相联系。
- 这部作品尤以其独特的文学形式，成为柏拉图最重要、最具影响力的作品之一。

定位

虽然柏拉图作品的创作顺序已经难以确定了，但通常认为《会饮篇》是柏拉图中期的作品，大约可追溯至公元前 380 年，那时柏拉图约 50 岁。[1] 在柏拉图很多早期的、关注伦理和正义问题的作品中，他借他的老师苏格拉底之口来表达那些声称拥有真知的人的设想与信念。

在这个时期，柏拉图的思考范围似乎已经拓展到多个主题，包括一个理想政体的建立（《理想国》）和灵魂的本质（《斐德若篇》）等。通常认为柏拉图的《吕西斯篇》创作于《会饮篇》之前，后者完善并发展了前者所讨论的主题——爱、欲望、教育与德性——并将其置于一个更加简短的文本中。[2]

在《斐德若篇》中，柏拉图再次探讨爱欲、美与知识的问题，并在书中更详细地论述了他的理念论以及知识是一种回忆的观点。一般认为《斐德若篇》作于《会饮篇》之后，它的观点与《会饮篇》的形成参照。例如，它将爱欲的迷狂视为一种力量，这种力量能够唤起人的灵魂在出世前所经历过的"理想形式"的记忆；此外，它还有利于人们获取德性。苏格拉底认为这种迷狂是"所有神圣占有的形式中最好的"。[3]

柏拉图《斐德若篇》中的苏格拉底认为，对肉体的欲求不仅是梯子上的一个台阶，在更高的台阶之上还有着更加崇高、更加抽象的有关爱与美的观念。[4] 人与人之间的关系本身就是有价值的。[5] 但应当注意到，柏拉图的两个最重要的政治作品，《理想国》及后来的《法篇》，在爱欲对于稳固城邦的作用这方面得出了不同的结论。[6]

> （《会饮篇》）对于爱情关系的本质与目标的探讨，带领我们理解柏拉图关于美好生活及其实现方式的观点核心。
> —— 弗里斯比·C.C.谢菲尔德："导读"，《柏拉图：〈会饮篇〉》

整合

柏拉图的哲学作品体系是哲学史上最重要的成就之一。这些作品互不相同并且难以统一，主要由对话构成，且很难对这些对话进行单一、权威的解读，《会饮篇》也只能被视为这一作品总集中的一个部分。

将柏拉图的所有作品视为一个整体来解读是数百年来学者们一直关注的问题，现代对于这个问题的讨论主要分为"演变论"*和"统一论"*两派。[7] 根据演变论的观点，柏拉图哲学在发展过程中采取了不同的心理学、认识论和伦理立场；而另一方面，根据"统一论"的观点，"柏拉图所有的对话能够体现出柏拉图学说或理念系统性的统一。"[8]

这些对立观点的存在，说明在柏拉图的著作中很难总结出一套清晰而系统的学说。《会饮篇》作为柏拉图中期的一部作品，描述了他在其他作品中探讨和论辩过的观点（其中包括理念论、爱欲与真理和正义的关系，以及我们对事物进行分类和逻辑推理的方式）。《会饮篇》是他所有对话作品中最具戏剧性和最详尽的，[9]在柏拉图的作品体系中它的独特意义在于其开创性的文学形式。

意义

柏拉图常被比作"西方哲学之父"。[10]作为柏拉图的代表作之一，《会饮篇》的意义不容置疑。从它最初在古典时期被接受（以及经常被模仿）到后来的基督教时代，它都被证明是一部具有卓越影响力的作品。它"塑造了人们想象古典时期雅典'黄金时代'的方式"[11]，直到今天还给学者们带来启发。

也许有些看似讽刺的是，使《会饮篇》从柏拉图其他作品中脱颖而出的特质，是其极具文学性的形式和对个人欲望的直接讨论，然而正是这些特质有时削弱了人们对于作品丰富的哲学内涵的理解："一些学者同时阅读《会饮篇》《斐德若篇》以及《理想国》，并将这三者视为柏拉图主义标志，但甚至连他们也难以避免在研究文本时采取一种高度筛选性的方法。"[12]

然而，近来的学者们试图说明《会饮篇》的中心思想如何与柏拉图的整体思想融为一体。这也使人们重新意识到，作品的核心要素"与标准的柏拉图式问题密切相关：与美好生活的本质、与德性，以及与德性的获得与传播方式密切相关"。[13]

1. K. 多弗，"柏拉图《会饮篇》的日期"，《明智》，1965 年第 10 期：第 2—20 页。
2. 参见凯瑟琳·皮克斯托克："转述的问题：柏拉图《吕西斯篇》与《会饮篇》中的友谊与哲学问题"，《新黑衣修士》第 82 卷，2001 年，第 525—540 页。
3. 柏拉图：《斐德若篇》，沃尔特·汉密尔顿译，伦敦：企鹅出版社，1973 年，第 56 页。
4. 柏拉图：《会饮篇》，第 49—50 页。
5. 柏拉图：《斐德若篇》，第 64—65 页；A. W. 普莱斯：《柏拉图和亚里士多德的爱与友谊》，牛津：牛津大学出版社，1989 年，第 85—88 页。
6. 史蒂文·伯格：《情欲与启蒙的沉醉：论柏拉图的〈会饮篇〉》，纽约州奥尔巴尼：纽约州立大学出版社，2010 年，第 153 页。
7. 威廉·普赖尔："发展主义"，选自《柏拉图指南》，杰拉尔德 A. 编，伦敦：绵延出版社，2012 年，第 288—289 页。
8. 威廉·普赖尔："发展主义"，第 288 页。
9. 弗里斯比·C. C. 谢菲尔德：《柏拉图的〈会饮篇〉：欲望伦理》，牛津：牛津大学出版社，2006 年，第 3 页。
10. A.N. 怀特海：《过程与实在：宇宙论研究》（修订版），纽约：自由出版社，1978 年，第 39 页。
11. 理查德·亨特：《柏拉图的〈会饮篇〉》，牛津：牛津大学出版社，2004 年，第 113 页。
12. 谢菲尔德：《柏拉图的〈会饮篇〉》，第 3 页。
13. 谢菲尔德：《柏拉图的〈会饮篇〉》，第 3 页。

第三部分：学术影响

9 最初反响

要点

- 与柏拉图不同,哲学家色诺芬*更强调爱欲的功能性;柏拉图的学生亚里士多德相较情欲之爱更加强调友谊之爱。
- 虽然无法得知柏拉图如何回应当时的批评,但可以说比起《会饮篇》,后来的《斐德若篇》对爱欲的叙述更多地涉及人际关系问题。
- 根据当时雅典的文化语境与柏拉图学园这个机构的学术背景,我们可以推论,《会饮篇》很可能是柏拉图生平被激烈讨论的主题。

批评

我们对于柏拉图《会饮篇》批判性回应的认识有限,因为我们无法确定作品具体的成书时间,以及我们很少能够从柏拉图的批评家那里得到明确的参考材料。尽管如此,我们还是可以大致划分出两种最初始的批判性回应。

第一种是哲学家色诺芬的《会饮篇》[1],其主要人物也是哲学家苏格拉底。在作品中,色诺芬让苏格拉底分享了他在爱欲、德性与和睦城邦生活方面的才智。

色诺芬笔下的苏格拉底以一个专业的调解者自居。我们能够看到,他的技能不论对于民众还是城邦的团结都是颇有裨益的。他可以"促进城邦间的友谊和安排合适的联姻,很适合作为国家或个人的盟友"。[2] 与柏拉图的作品相似,色诺芬也透过幽默和讽刺论述哲学——但色诺芬作了一些关键性的修改,因此也暗含了他对柏拉图观点的批判。

虽然他承认爱欲在精神方面超过了肉体，但却选择强调其"次要"形式的实际价值："友爱"（即友情的力量，或与友情相关的爱的力量）。为了这样做，他提出了自己对爱的设想，与柏拉图笔下的苏格拉底相比，他所提出的爱是更为个人化和互惠的*——据说对城邦也更加有益。

第二种对柏拉图《会饮篇》最初的批判性回应见于他早期的学生亚里士多德的《尼各马可伦理学》，它间接回应了柏拉图关于爱欲与德性的理论。亚里士多德淡化了爱欲对于哲学实践与德性生活的意义。在他看来，爱欲是一种不稳定的力量，是"一种过度的感觉"[3]。他认为，尽管它能够在两个人之间建立起完美的友情，但却因为过于强烈而不能在多人间分享。相反，亚里士多德强调不那么强烈的更具有互惠性的"友爱"："好人和在德性上相似的人之间的友爱"。[4] 爱欲与过剩相关，而友爱则更像是一种"性格状态"[5]。选用友爱作为纽带，将民众与城邦在共同的德性上相连结，亚里士多德——与色诺芬一样——反对柏拉图在《会饮篇》中借苏格拉底之口提出的爱欲的概念，其更加抽象、更加先验。[6]

> 就拥有完美的友谊关系而言，一个人不可能是许多人的朋友，正如一个人不能同时与许多人处于爱（欲）关系中（因为爱（欲）是一种感情上的过度，而由于其性质，这种感觉只能对一个人产生）。
>
> —— 亚里士多德：《尼各马可伦理学》

回应

由于缺少柏拉图同当时的受众直接接触的文字证据，我们很难确定柏拉图如何回应那些针对他的批评者们。

鉴于柏拉图学园是一个学习的场所,并且雅典的知识文化以激烈的论辩为特点,我们可以假定关于柏拉图《会饮篇》的批判性对话和其对爱欲的讨论着实发生过——即使我们永远也不会知道它的详细过程。然而,我们可以通过观察柏拉图在这之后的作品中论述爱欲时的变化来推测这些论辩的性质(尽管我们必须小心,不要绝对地宣称这些变动是由作者与批评者之间的对话导致的)。

通常认为柏拉图的《斐德若篇》作于《会饮篇》之后,因而它很适合用来考察这些问题。虽然这篇对话也研究了爱欲与友爱对追求智慧与德性的作用,但柏拉图对于爱欲的论述已经和《会饮篇》不同了。在《斐德若篇》里,爱欲仍然能够驱动并且激发真知的发展,但与苏格拉底在《会饮篇》中所声称的不同,爱欲的存在并不是为了引导爱人从关注他所爱的肉体转向凝视超验的美。这样,不论是爱还是被爱都同样通往真理。就如柏拉图所解释的那样,被爱者"经历了一种'反向的爱',这是他所激发的爱的反映"。[7]

尽管这似乎预示着亚里士多德在《尼各马可伦理学》中所强调的:完美的爱是相互的——在两个人之间分享[8]——但柏拉图在《斐德若篇》中的观点与亚里士多德的不同。柏拉图认为爱欲的"迷狂"通过伦理上的启发而催生德性。然而,亚里士多德不信任这种"过度"的情欲之爱。[9]

冲突与共识

柏拉图与亚里士多德对理想形式的爱及其对追求智慧与德性所起的作用有不同的看法,这一直以来都为学者所研究,至今仍是如此。柏拉图和亚里士多德最根本的分歧在于他们赋予爱欲的意义[10]——一个历史上形形色色的思想家始终感兴趣的论题。例如，早期的基督教神学家圣奥古斯丁借鉴了柏拉图对美的提升的描述，把欲望作为他的爱的神学的中心。[11]最近，教皇本笃十六世*在其2005年爱的通谕（通谕是教皇写给罗马天主教*所有主教的信）中提到了《会饮篇》。[12]尽管以一种基督化的形式，他也强调了情欲之爱对追求智慧与真理的意义。

现代的柏拉图研究者们也试图充分理解柏拉图在《会饮篇》中所强调的爱欲。[13]可以说，对作品这一方面的认识已经界定了对它的批评接受，并且它很可能还将继续是作品最受争议的特质。

---

1. 色诺芬：《苏格拉底的对话》，休·特里德尼克和罗宾·沃特菲尔德译，伦敦：企鹅出版社，1990年。
2. 色诺芬：《苏格拉底的对话》，第251页。
3. 亚里士多德：《尼各马可伦理学》，戴维·罗斯译，牛津：牛津大学出版社，1980年，第201页。
4. 亚里士多德：《尼各马可伦理学》，第196页。
5. 亚里士多德：《尼各马可伦理学》，第200页。
6. 理查德·克劳特："导论"，《亚里士多德〈尼各马伦理学〉布莱克威尔指南》，理查德·克劳特编，牛津：布莱克威尔出版社，2006年，第9页。
7. 柏拉图：《斐德若篇》，沃尔特·汉密尔顿译，伦敦：企鹅出版社，1973年，第64页。
8. A. W. 普莱斯：《柏拉图和亚里士多德的爱与友谊》，牛津：牛津大学出版社，1989年，第85—86页；凯瑟琳·皮克斯托克："转述的问题：柏拉图《吕西斯篇》与《会饮篇》中的友谊与哲学问题"，《新黑衣修士》第82卷，2001年，第 525—540 页。
9. 柏拉图:《斐德若篇》,第 56 页;亚里士多德:《尼各马可伦理学》,第 201 页。
10. 参见普莱斯:《柏拉图和亚里士多德的爱与友谊》。
11. 伯纳德·V.布拉迪:《基督之爱》,华盛顿特区:乔治敦大学出版社,2003 年,第 79 页。
12. 本笃十六世:《天主是爱》(基督之爱的通谕),2005 年 12 月 25 日,第 11 条。
13. 弗里斯比·C.C.谢菲尔德:《柏拉图的〈会饮篇〉:欲望伦理》,牛津:牛津大学出版社,2006 年;史蒂文·伯格:《情欲与启蒙的沉醉:论柏拉图的〈会饮篇〉》,纽约州奥尔巴尼:纽约州立大学出版社,2010 年;加里·艾伦·斯科特和威廉·A.威尔顿:《情欲的智慧:柏拉图〈会饮篇〉中的哲学与媒介性》,纽约州奥尔巴尼:纽约州立大学出版社,2008 年。

10. 后续争议

要点 🔑

- 《会饮篇》成为一种新型哲学写作的灵感来源。
- 这篇对话对西方思想和文化的巨大影响可在西方的哲学、神学、文学和诗学中看到。
- 作品重新探讨了爱、欲望、德性、性别与性欲,如今它依旧影响着有关这些主题的讨论。

应用与问题

柏拉图《会饮篇》独特的文学形式对后来的作家尤其具有启发性。将一场宴会作为讨论哲学思想的文学背景,这种创意是如此地令人惊奇,以至于长期以来都不乏模仿者。诚然,柏拉图的作品被称为"(一种)文类的经典创始文本"。[1]

我们也许还需要感谢《会饮篇》,因为作品中那些生动、诙谐的人物的发言启发了古典小说的写作。在公元1世纪罗马的讽刺作家佩特洛尼乌斯*的作品《萨蒂利孔》中,在一场丰盛的晚宴上我们读到一个单相思的故事,这不禁让我们忆起柏拉图《会饮篇》中阿尔西比亚德斯的言论。[2] 与之类似的还有公元2世纪阿基琉斯·塔提奥斯*的《琉基佩与克勒托丰》和阿普列尤斯*的《变形记》,它们改编了柏拉图的创意以适应不同的受众,特别是用异性恋的欲望与伦理模式替代了相对应的同性恋模式。[3]

作品的核心问题——爱欲对追求智慧与德性的作用——对后来被统称为"希腊化(哲学)*"的哲学流派仍然很重要。芝诺*及其他早期斯多葛学派*哲学家都强调爱欲有益伦理。斯多葛学派的哲学家认为最好的德性生活是与自然和谐共处，至于痛苦还是欢乐，他们并不关心。斯多葛学派试图"通过进一步结合爱欲同教育，改善柏拉图在《会饮篇》中提出的爱欲概念"。[4] 基督教的思想家们之后发展了这一主题。

对柏拉图《会饮篇》的基督教解读可追溯至普罗提诺——公元 3 世纪的"新柏拉图主义"哲学家。新柏拉图主义是神秘主义的哲学和宗教体系，深受柏拉图作品的影响。普罗提诺为后来的基督教传统奠定了基础，即将美的提升视为基督教灵魂升天的异教对等物。[5]

在公元 3 至 5 世纪，早期的神学家如亚历山大的奥利金*、尼撒的贵格利*和希波的奥古斯丁根据基督教的语境对柏拉图关于爱欲的观点进行改编。例如，奥古斯丁对爱的阐释就受到了"美的提升"相关段落的强烈影响，这一形象奠定了他爱的神学的基础。[6] 在欧洲文艺复兴时期（约 14 至 16 世纪），意大利的莱昂纳多·布鲁尼*翻译了柏拉图的《会饮篇》。他的译本删去了原本对爱欲偏色情和露骨的描写，而天主教学者马尔西利奥·费奇诺深受这个译本的影响，对《会饮篇》进行了适合基督教的改写，删除了一些内容，意义深远。[7]

> 《会饮篇》为后世所有描写文学晚宴的文本奠定了基础。
>
> ——理查德·亨特：《柏拉图的〈会饮篇〉》

思想流派

柏拉图的观点对整个西方思想文化都有着深刻的影响，尤其因为它通过希波的奥古斯丁等人的作品进入了基督教神学领域。从文艺复兴时期开始，随着艺术家与知识分子的关注，这些观点开始重新以自己的方式广泛地传播。19世纪的诗人，如珀西·比希·雪莱*，借柏拉图对于爱欲的论述来界定浪漫的爱情。[8]20世纪的主要作家也直接借鉴柏拉图的《会饮篇》。E.M.福斯特*在他的小说《莫瑞斯》中用《会饮篇》来探讨同性恋的问题，小说将柏拉图作为一面透视镜，透过他来考察爱欲的精神与肉体概念，就像苏格拉底与阿尔西比亚德斯这组对立的人物所分别体现的那样。[9]

进入20世纪和21世纪，各流派的哲学家们都在不断重提柏拉图，包括马丁·海德格尔*、雅克·德里达*、米歇尔·福柯*等大陆哲学家*。[10]分析哲学*流派的现代柏拉图主义者采用逻辑和科学的方式分析哲学问题，他们的认识论取向（专注于知识的本质和范围及其获取）来自柏拉图的"真、善、美理念"。这种理论将这些理念归为超验的特征，它们的存在超出那些世上我们可以用感官感知的事物——"可感知的"对象。

戈特洛布·弗雷格*、伯特兰·罗素*、希拉里·普特南*以及最近的索尔·克里普克*等哲学家在不同程度上都持有该观点，认为可感知的对象是这些抽象形式的变体。[11]

《会饮篇》中的观点也被精神分析*理论家如西格蒙德·弗洛伊德*和雅克·拉康*等借鉴，用以阐释欲望的概念。[12]影视、艺术和戏剧也常常用到《会饮篇》，如彼得·保罗·鲁本斯*的画作，描绘了阿尔西比亚德斯戏剧性地造访柏拉图晚宴的那个时刻，[13]还有电影《摇滚芭比》*（2001），涉及阿里斯托芬所说的神话，有关人类欲望以及与另一半相结合的渴望。

当代研究

柏拉图的《会饮篇》对当代学术研究仍然有着广泛的影响。古典哲学家、柏拉图研究者[14],以及基督教神学家们毫无意外地仍然在讨论并分析着柏拉图的作品。[15]罗兰·巴特等文学理论家在柏拉图的作品中也发现了很多有趣的东西,尤其是文本开放式结尾的结构以及谈话者之间复杂且含混的互动。[16]

当代性别和性理论家如大卫·霍尔朴林*注意到作品中阿里斯托芬对性的不同寻常的见解。[17]这引发了争论,即关于柏拉图的古典文本在多大程度上可以作为当代性别规范和性偏好的范本。霍尔朴林本人一直热衷于强调,现代人对性取向的理解并不符合古希腊那种更为灵活的性观念。例如,几乎没有证据表明古希腊有明确的同性恋文化,精英男士(如柏拉图在《会饮篇》中所描述的那些)认为,与男性发生性关系并不妨碍他们为了传宗接代而与女性结婚。[18]

霍尔朴林还说到,阿里斯托芬的演讲"没有从他所讲述的神话中得出同性恋与异性恋的区别,正是他的分析逻辑不可避免地导致了这个结果。这个遗漏很能说明问题"。[19]这是一场重要的、持续的论辩。

---

1. 理查德·亨特:《柏拉图的〈会饮篇〉》,牛津:牛津大学出版社,2004年,第15页。

2. 亨特:《柏拉图的〈会饮篇〉》,第 126 页。
3. 亨特:《柏拉图的〈会饮篇〉》,第 122—123 和 127—129 页。
4. 伯纳德·科莱特-杜契奇:"交友:斯多葛的爱情观及其柏拉图背景",选自《古典时期和中世纪的友谊观》,苏珊娜·斯特恩-吉利特和加里·M. 居特勒编,纽约州奥尔巴尼:纽约州立大学出版社,2014 年,第 108 页。
5. 普罗提诺:"爱",选自《九章集》,斯蒂芬·麦克纳译,伦敦:企鹅出版社,1991 年,第 174—186 页;亨特:《柏拉图的〈会饮篇〉》,第 130—131 页。
6. 伯纳德·V. 布拉迪:《基督之爱》,华盛顿特区:乔治敦大学出版社,2003 年,第 79 页。
7. 马尔西利奥·费奇诺:《论柏拉图式的爱——柏拉图〈会饮〉义疏》,西尔斯·杰恩译,得克萨斯州达拉斯:春季出版物,1985 年;亨特:《柏拉图的〈会饮篇〉》,第 134 页。
8. 亨特:《柏拉图的〈会饮篇〉》,第 123—124 页。
9. E. M. 福斯特:《莫瑞斯》,伦敦:企鹅出版社,2005 年;亨特:《柏拉图的〈会饮篇〉》,第 115—117 页。
10. 有关摘要,请参见德鲁·海兰:《质疑柏拉图主义:大陆哲学对柏拉图的阐释》,纽约州奥尔巴尼:纽约州立大学出版社,2004 年。
11. 见马克·巴拉格尔:"形而上学中的柏拉图主义",《斯坦福大学哲学百科全书》,2014 年春季版,爱德华·N. 扎尔塔编,登录日期 2015 年 4 月 1 日,http://plato.stanford.edu/archives/spr2014/entries/platonism/。
12. 西格蒙德·弗洛伊德:《超越快乐原则》,詹姆斯·斯特雷奇译,伦敦和纽约:诺顿出版公司,1961 年,第 52 页;雅克·拉康:《选集:英文第一版》,布鲁斯·芬克译,纽约和伦敦:诺顿出版公司,2006 年,第 699—700 页;亨特:《柏拉图的〈会饮篇〉》,第 117—119 页。
13. 伊丽莎白·麦格拉思:"'醉汉的偏见':鲁本斯关于柏拉图〈会饮篇〉的绘画",《瓦尔堡和考陶尔德学院学报》第 46 卷,1983 年,第 228—235 页。
14. 见亨特:《柏拉图的〈会饮篇〉》;弗里斯比·C. C. 谢菲尔德:《柏拉图的〈会饮篇〉:欲望伦理》,牛津:牛津大学出版社,2006 年;史蒂文·伯格:《情欲与启蒙的沉醉:论柏拉图的〈会饮篇〉》,纽约州奥尔巴尼:纽约州立大学出版社,2010 年。
15. 见凯瑟琳·皮克斯托克:《转述的问题:柏拉图〈吕西斯篇〉与〈会饮篇〉中的友谊与哲学问题》,《新黑衣修士》第 82 卷,2001 年,第 525—540 页;本笃十六世：《天主是爱》，基督之爱的通谕，2005年12月25日，第11条。
16. 亨特：《柏拉图的〈会饮篇〉》，第113页；罗兰·巴特：《恋人絮语》，理查德·霍华德译，伦敦：佳酿出版社，2002年；也见：杰弗里·卡恩斯："不是一个神话：柏拉图〈会饮篇〉的话语建构"，选自《重新思考性：福柯与古典时期》，大卫·H.J.拉莫尔等编，新泽西州普林斯顿：普林斯顿大学出版社，1998年，第104—121页。
17. 见大卫·霍尔朴林："柏拉图与情欲叙事"，选自《古典的革新》，丹尼尔·塞尔登和拉尔夫·赫克斯特编，纽约：劳德里奇出版社，1992年，第95—126页。
18. 大卫·霍尔朴林：《同性恋一百年：和其他关于古希腊爱情的论文》，伦敦：劳德里奇出版社，1990年，第15—40页。
19. 霍尔朴林：《同性恋一百年》，第18—19页。

11 当代印迹

要点 🔑

- 《会饮篇》是西方哲学的经典文本之一。
- 柏拉图在论述爱时强调爱欲，这对当代的思想家来说仍然是一个具有挑战性的论题。
- 批评者认为柏拉图所论述的爱并不是足够互惠的，其留给纯粹情感的空间太少了。

地位

在很大程度上，《会饮篇》为柏拉图赢取了"西方哲学之父"的美誉，这是一部不论在哲学还是文学上都颇具创见的作品。[1] 鉴于两千余年来，这部作品对西方思想文化产生了广泛影响，所以学者们不断重提这个文本就不足为奇。文本的接受史和它所反映的有关作者及其生活年代的信息，在不同方面引起人们的兴趣。

也许更应该令人惊讶的是，现代各学科的学者们仍在不同程度上创造性地用到这部作品。精神分析学家[2]、后结构主义*文学批评家、[3]性别与性理论家[4]在近几十年来都转向这部作品，有时他们的研究涉及哲学和神学等更加"传统的"领域。此类研究运用不同学科的方法和理论，被称为"跨学科"研究。一个跨学科研究的例子是，一位基督教神学家近来借鉴文学分析的方法来探究《会饮篇》复杂的结构方式，这种谋篇布局是为了提醒受众"我们获得的真理的不牢靠性和偏颇性"。[5]

该文本今日仍然具有现实性意义，这一点最近在美国科罗拉多州的一个法庭案件中得到了证实。学者被召集讨论《会饮篇》的同性恋观点,这是当今宪法的*修正案和同性恋者权利相关案例的一部分。6

> 欧洲哲学传统最确当的一般特征是,它由对柏拉图的一系列脚注构成。
> —— A.N. 怀特海:《过程与实在:宇宙论研究》

互动

《会饮篇》仍在哲学家与神学家之间引发争论,争论的焦点在于它对于情欲之爱的论述是否给人与人之间的情感留有空间(例如古典学研究者格雷戈里·弗拉斯托斯*最近提出的一个观点)7,或者它所认可的那种爱的形式是否有些缺乏人情味。

这些论争的根源真的很古老——柏拉图和亚里士多德对究竟是什么构成了理想形式的爱持有不同观点:亚里士多德支持友爱(更强调互惠的友谊之爱),而柏拉图则偏向爱欲。但柏拉图在分析爱时强调爱欲,这仍然与当代思想相冲突。例如,丹麦神学家虞格仁*驳斥柏拉图式的爱(以及古希腊泛指的爱欲),他认为其从根本上说是贪婪的——即"自私自利的"。8

凯瑟琳·奥斯本等学者为柏拉图辩护,认为柏拉图对爱欲的论述实际上为构建人际间丰富的爱之形式提供了基础,从而使柏拉图免受弗拉斯托斯和虞格仁等人的批判。9 凯瑟琳·皮克斯托克认为,要欣赏作品的这个方面,就必须注意到柏拉图使用的"不同寻常的'文学'手段"10,而这些常常为批评家们所忽略。她认为,批评家们对于文本的解读过于注重字面意思,而没有领会到文本不连贯的叙述形式对其意义的重要性。着重考虑文本本身的结构，可以让我们看到，对柏拉图来说，"友谊本身就被建构为一系列友好的沟通交流"。[11]

持续争议

对柏拉图所述的情欲之爱的批评直接涉及他的文本，并且这些批评同样反对那些受他影响的思想传统。对于第一种直接涉及《会饮篇》的情况，格雷戈里·弗拉斯托斯认为柏拉图所表达的个人之爱仅仅是一种手段，目的是使人达到更高的境界，特别是对美本身的凝视（弗拉斯托斯从苏格拉底关于"美的提升"的发言中得出此观点）。因此，人类仅仅被看作工具，被看作"谓词'有用的'和'漂亮的'的占位符"，并且，柏拉图在他自己的等级制度中"将对人的爱放在了最低的层次"。[12] 弗拉斯托斯接着谈到了亚里士多德对于理想之爱的论述，他说，亚里士多德告诉我们："爱一个人就是为了这个人的缘故而希望他好"。[13] 弗拉斯托斯认为亚里士多德的观点远胜于柏拉图的。

而虞格仁的批判则集中于古希腊关于爱欲的一般概念以及那些基督教神学形式，它们以柏拉图为基础，试图在他们的爱情神学中为爱欲找到核心地位。虞格仁认为爱欲在根本上是"以自我为中心的"，或者说是自私私立的，并且视其为一种极其不充分的爱的形式。[14] 相反，在他看来，真正的爱能净化任何追逐私利的动机。因此，他反对强调爱欲的基督教神学形式，捍卫一种另类的神学，其将自我牺牲的爱阐释为唯一"真正的"基督之爱。[15]

1. 理查德·亨特：《柏拉图的〈会饮篇〉》，牛津：牛津大学出版社，2004年，第113页。
2. 亨特：《柏拉图的〈会饮篇〉》，第117—119页。
3. 夏伦·贝尔："圣妓之墓：《会饮篇》"，选自《精神的暗影：后现代主义与宗教》，菲利普·贝里和安德鲁·韦尼克编，伦敦：劳德里奇出版社，1992年，第198—210页；保罗·艾伦·米勒："后结构主义的古典根源：拉康、德里达和福柯"，《国际古典传统期刊》第5卷，1998年，第209—213页。
4. 大卫·霍尔朴林："柏拉图与情欲叙事"，选自《古典的革新》，丹尼尔·塞尔登和拉尔夫·赫克斯特编，纽约：劳德里奇出版社，1992年，第95—126页；杰弗里·卡恩斯："不是一个神话：柏拉图〈会饮篇〉的话语建构"，选自《重新思考性：福柯与古典时期》，大卫·H. J. 拉莫尔等编，新泽西州普林斯顿：普林斯顿大学出版社，1998年，第104—121页。
5. 凯瑟琳·皮克斯托克："转述的问题：柏拉图《吕西斯篇》与《会饮篇》中的友谊与哲学问题"，《新黑衣修士》第82卷，2001年，第525—540页。
6. 亨特：《柏拉图的〈会饮篇〉》，第125页；玛莎·努斯鲍姆："柏拉图式的爱与科罗拉多法律：古希腊规范与现代性争议的关联"，《弗吉尼亚法律评论》第80卷，1994年，第1515—1651页。
7. 格雷戈里·弗拉斯托斯："柏拉图以个人为爱的对象"，选自《柏拉图主义研究》，格雷戈里·弗拉斯托斯编，新泽西州普林斯顿：普林斯顿大学出版社，1973年，第3—42页。
8. 虞格仁：《圣爱与爱欲》，菲利·普沃森译，伦敦：SPCK出版社，1983年。
9. 凯瑟琳·奥斯本《柏拉图与上帝之爱》，牛津：克拉伦登出版社，1994年，第222—226页；也见皮克斯托克："转述的问题"，第525—540页。
10. 皮克斯托克："转述的问题"，第526页。
11. 皮克斯托克："转述的问题"，第530页。
12. 弗拉斯托斯："柏拉图以个人为爱的对象"，第26页。
13. 弗拉斯托斯："柏拉图以个人为爱的对象"，第3页。
14. 虞格仁：《圣爱与爱欲》，第210页。
15. 虞格仁：《圣爱与爱欲》，第559—560和721页。

12 未来展望

要点

- 作为西方哲学的基础文本,《会饮篇》的重要性不会降低。
- 作品对爱欲的强调、复杂的叙述结构和关于性别与性的独创思想持续激发学者们的兴趣。
- 文本惊人的哲学见解、文学方面的原创性以及在西方文明中的接受方式,使我们必须将其视为一部开创性的著作。

潜力

柏拉图的《会饮篇》是西方文学的一部开创性作品,并且极有可能持续具有价值意义。在《会饮篇》诞生大约 2 500 年后,人们依然热衷于讨论这部作品,以更好地理解古希腊及其文化关怀,以及柏拉图的思想如何塑造爱、欲望与伦理的相关理论。例如,当我们研究许多世纪以来人们如何运用《会饮篇》来解释上帝之爱是人与人之间爱的典范时,我们在了解文本的同时也了解了欧洲的文化史。

研究柏拉图的学者、哲学家和神学家们依然在参考这部作品,试图解答它所提出的一些问题,关于爱欲以及理想形式的爱。但《会饮篇》对于西方文化的渗透性影响已经远远超出学术问题的范围。我们可以从对爱与欲望的文化假设,以及这些东西与智慧、德性和幸福的关系中看到这一点。我们已经知道《会饮篇》如何塑造了诗与文学、视觉艺术与电影之间的关系。

此外,近一个世纪以来,精神分析学家如西格蒙德·弗洛伊德和雅克·拉康，后结构主义文学理论家如罗兰·巴特，性别与性理论家如米歇尔·福柯和大卫·霍尔朴林都对文本进行了创造性的运用。

运用精巧的文学手段来表达深刻的哲学观点，这让《会饮篇》成为一个复杂而深奥的文本，在许多语境中都极具启发性。作为柏拉图文学和哲学独特天资的代表性象征，只要西方文明不断审视过去以理解自身，《会饮篇》就将继续被视为一部重要的作品。

> 柏拉图的《会饮篇》对现代读者来说有着独特的吸引力。可以说，柏拉图其他的对话都不能在论述柏拉图思想中如此重要的主题同时，如此戏剧性地描述著名的古典人物。
>
> —— 加里·艾伦·斯科特和威廉 A. 威尔顿：
> 《情欲的智慧：柏拉图〈会饮篇〉中的哲学与媒介性》

未来方向

新一代的柏拉图研究者们正在重新探讨柏拉图强调爱欲的意义，并重新阐释作品对于古希腊和当代世界的意义。[1] 有些人认为作品不同寻常的文学特征是解读文本的关键。[2] 此外，一些对文本最具创见性的回应来自文学、性别和性理论家。法国文化理论家米歇尔·福柯于 1980 年代初期出版了著名的《性史》三卷本，它使得很多学者回归古典时期的论题，特别是柏拉图的《会饮篇》，福柯在《性史》的第二卷论述了这个问题。[3] 这些学者的目的是厘清、论争并且研究福柯的理论框架与成果。

柏拉图在对话中借阿里斯托芬之口提出的欲望理论（即其提及的神话：人类曾被一分为二而导致如今被重新聚合的欲望所驱使）

已经成为争论的焦点。⁴ 柏拉图认为，我们的性取向取决于我们被分裂前的整体构成（男-女、男-男或女-女），这成为现代性学理论家素所热衷的议题。比如，美国作家大卫·霍尔朴林的《同性恋一百年》是一部讨论古希腊性观念的论文集。⁵

阿里斯托芬关于灵魂分裂的神话与多个问题相关，包括近来更多有关性与性别认同的讨论，我们的性别究竟在多大程度上由文化塑造以及生物决定论*与社会建构论*。生物决定论认为人类个体的特征由基因决定，社会建构论认为包括性取向在内的人类价值观和偏好由其所处的社会和文化环境决定。有人认为《会饮篇》远比人们可能认识到的要激进，也许它使"性"转变"为哲学的一种形式"，从而使"我们与柏拉图一起，也为了柏拉图而将性重塑。"⁶

同样地，女性主义思想家也阅读柏拉图的《会饮篇》以寻求对女性性欲更有力的认可。有人认为，柏拉图提出了一种更为包容的女性观以及一种可能有助于认识女性的视角，即女性文化所决定的女性权利的"缺失"不能用来定义女性。⁷ 根据这种观点，柏拉图为性理论铺平了道路，这可能有助于我们驳斥那些在他之后出现的性与性别模式。

小结

柏拉图的《会饮篇》催生了一种新的哲学文学：在庄谐参半的晚宴上，人们以一种轻松愉快的方式讨论重大的哲学问题。这种文学形式从古至今都不乏模仿者。⁸ 在对苏格拉底、阿里斯托芬、阿尔西比亚德斯等著名历史人物鲜活、生动的刻画之中，存在着哲学思辨、人类性欲的神话以及对爱欲与伦理关系的考察。这些问题在几千年来一直吸引着读者与批评家。

《会饮篇》是一部包含柏拉图最优秀文学手法的作品，它将隐喻、戏仿、清晰的推理和修辞技巧结合在一起。柏拉图其他作品所蕴含的哲学观点，在这部作品中以一种不同寻常的抒情方式得以展示，比如有关"可理解的形式"*的理论，这种形式存在于我们能用感官感知的世界之外。柏拉图借苏格拉底发表的，关于从对肉体的爱欲到看见抽象的"美的理念"的精神旅程，对绝大部分的西方文化尤其是基督教思想和文化产生了深远的影响。

　　《会饮篇》的意义远不止柏拉图的思想以及他表达这些思想的形式，多年来人们对这部作品的接受以及它对整个西方文明的影响深度，使它仍然是有史以来艺术和人文领域最伟大的作品之一。

---

1. 见弗里斯比·C. C. 谢菲尔德：《柏拉图的〈会饮篇〉：欲望伦理》，牛津：牛津大学出版社，2006 年；史蒂文·伯格：《情欲与启蒙的沉醉：论柏拉图的〈会饮篇〉》，纽约州奥尔巴尼：纽约州立大学出版社，2010 年；加里·艾伦·斯科特和威廉·A. 威尔顿：《情欲的智慧：柏拉图〈会饮篇〉中的哲学与媒介性》，纽约州奥尔巴尼：纽约州立大学出版社，2008 年。
2. 见凯瑟琳·皮克斯托克：《转述的问题：柏拉图〈吕西斯篇〉与〈会饮篇〉中的友谊与哲学问题》，《新黑衣修士》第 82 卷，2001 年，第 125—140 页。
3. 米歇尔·福柯：《快感的享用》，选自《性史》第二卷，罗伯特·赫利译，纽约：兰登书屋，1990 年，第 230—233 和 235—242 页。
4. 柏拉图：《会饮篇》，选自《柏拉图：〈会饮篇〉》，M.C. 豪瓦斯顿译，M.C. 豪瓦斯顿与弗里斯比·C. C. 谢菲尔德编，剑桥：剑桥大学出版社，2008 年，第 22—27 页。
5. 大卫·霍尔朴林：《同性恋一百年：和其他关于古希腊爱情的论文》，伦敦：劳特利奇出版社，1990 年，第 15—40 页；杰弗里·卡恩斯：《不是一个神话：柏拉图〈会饮篇〉的话语建构》，选自《重新思考性：福柯与古典时期》，大卫·H. J. 拉莫尔等编，新泽西州普林斯顿：普林斯顿大学出版社，1998年，第104—121页。

6. 卡恩斯:《不是一个神话》，第120页。
7. 夏伦·贝尔："圣妓之墓：《会饮篇》"，选自《精神的暗影：后现代主义与宗教》，菲利普·贝里和安德鲁·韦尼克编，伦敦：劳德里奇出版社，1992年，第198—210页；安妮·玛丽·鲍里："狄欧蒂玛给苏格拉底讲的故事：柏拉图〈会饮篇〉的叙事分析"，选自《女性主义与古代哲学》，朱莉·K.沃德编，伦敦：劳德里奇出版社，1996年，第175—194页。
8. 理查德·亨特:《柏拉图的〈会饮篇〉》，牛津：牛津大学出版社，2004年，第9—10页。

术语表

1. **柏拉图学园**：公元前387年，柏拉图在雅典城外建立的一个有影响的哲学学校，此地因是古代英雄阿卡德摩斯的埋藏地而被视为神圣之地。其兴盛一直持续到大约公元前87年。

2. **分析哲学**：当代哲学的一个分支，它被认为在英美哲学研究中占主导地位，在哲学风格和方法论上常常与"大陆哲学"形成对比。它用逻辑和科学的方法来解决哲学问题，强调对信息的验证必须采用来自数理逻辑学的严密证明。

3. **古典时期**：古代历史的一个时间段，特指中世纪以前的"古典"文明，尤其指古希腊和古罗马的文明。

4. **美的提升**：柏拉图认为，爱欲能激起我们一种向上攀爬的欲望，就像我们站在梯子上一样，从看到美丽的肉体，到看到永恒的美的理念本身。向美攀登的第一级"阶梯"是对某一个美丽肉体的爱；中间阶段是对所有美丽肉体的欣赏、对美丽灵魂的爱、对制度与律法之美的爱以及对知识之美的爱；最后一级阶梯则是看到美的理念本身及其所带来的真正的德行。

5. **生物决定论**：该理论认为人类个体特征，包括性取向和其他偏好是由基因决定的。

6. **基督教**：以耶稣基督和《圣经》教义为基础的全球性宗教。基督教、犹太教和伊斯兰教是三大"一神教"（信仰一神的）宗教体系。

7. **公民身份**：确定居住在城市的人的地位和义务的那些东西（在此书中，城市指古雅典的城邦）。

8. **宪法的**：关于一个国家或国家治理的一套既定原则（如美国宪法）。

9. **大陆哲学**：当代哲学分支，20世纪在欧洲大陆占主导地位，在风格和方法上通常与英美哲学中占主导地位的"分析哲学"有所区别。

10. **神灵**：在古希腊思想和信仰中，神灵是一种超自然的中介性存在，常常在神与人之间进行沟通交流。

11. **演变论**：一种学术观点，认为柏拉图的哲学是在他修改自身哲学和心理学立场的过程中逐渐演变、发展起来的。

12. **论辩**：通过辩论赢得公众所需的技术和技巧。

13. **厄琉息斯秘仪**：在古希腊的厄琉息斯举行的秘密宗教仪式，始于对得墨忒耳和珀耳塞福涅女神的崇拜。

14. **史诗**：在古代文学中，以诗歌形式叙述与英雄人物有关的故事或传说的长诗。

15. **伊壁鸠鲁学派**：一个古老的哲学流派，哲学家伊壁鸠鲁在雅典创立，认为世界是由偶然统治的，把简单的快乐形式看作是最高的善。

16. **认识论**：哲学的分支学科，涉及知识的本质和范围以及获取知识的方法。

17. **含混的**：可解释的；模棱两可的。爱欲被认为是一种"含混的"力量，因为很难确定它的影响是正面还是负面的。

18. **爱欲**：古希腊语中与性欲有关的爱的形式，现代词语"色情的"由此而来。

19. **民族志**：对民族和文化的科学描述，包括他们的风俗习惯和独特的观念。

20. **美的理念**：美的永恒不变的"本质"，柏拉图称之为"奇妙的幻象"。美的理念的观照产生了真正的德性。

21. **享乐主义**：一种伦理学说或理论，其将快乐视为主要的善或合适的行为目的。

22. **《摇滚芭比》**：拍摄于2001年的美国电影，曾经获奖，由约翰·卡梅隆·米切尔导演，改编自他自己的舞台剧。这部电影经常提到阿里斯托芬在《会饮篇》中的言论。

23. **希腊化哲学**：亚里士多德之后在希腊（古希腊）文明中产生的各种思想流派，包括斯多葛学派、伊壁鸠鲁主义，以新柏拉图主义结束。

24. **荷鲁斯**：在古埃及神话中保护君主制的神，常被描绘成一个长着猎鹰头的人。

25. **可理解的形式**：能被智力感知并构成人类理解的思想。

26. **形而上学**：研究现实基本结构的哲学分支。

27. **神秘主义的**：关于宗教神秘主义的，即宗教信仰、实践或经验的精神形式，据说该主义超出了一般人的理解。

28. **新柏拉图主义**：公元3世纪的一个宗教和哲学流派，源于柏拉图哲学和各种神秘主义传统的结合。

29. **伯罗奔尼撒战争**：公元前431年至公元前404年，斯巴达城邦与雅典及其各自帝国之间的战争，以斯巴达人的胜利告终。

30. **复调**：用来描述《会饮篇》中"许多声音"的效果的术语。

31. **多神信仰**：崇拜或相信不止一个神。

32. **后结构主义**：20世纪的一种哲学和文学批评体系。后结构主义者反对"结构主义"的理论立场，即文本的意义存在于明确的叙述、解释和语言结构中。

33. **精神分析**：由西格蒙德·弗洛伊德发展起来的一种心理理论，由一种试图接近和解释无意识的治疗方法来定义。

34. **毕达哥拉斯学派**：源自古希腊哲学家和数学家毕达哥拉斯（公元前570—495年）教学的哲学和宗教的思想与实践体系，其基本思想是现实在本质上是数学的。

35. **互惠的**：通过回报完成的或与交换有关的。

36. **修辞学**：话语的艺术，或有说服力的说话和写作方式的艺术。一门指导学生有效使用语言的学科。古典时期至今，在欧洲的知识传统中占有中心地位。

37. **罗马天主教**：世界上最大的基督教和最古老的宗教组织之一，由教皇领导。

38. **亦庄亦谐的（悲喜剧的）**：结合了严肃和喜剧元素的文学类型。

39. **西勒诺斯**：古希腊宗教中的一个小辅神，与主神狄俄尼索斯和跳舞酿酒的活动有关。

40. **社会建构论**：一种理论，认为人的价值观和偏好包括性取向，是由一个人所处的社会和文化环境所决定的。

41. **智者**：古希腊哲学和修辞学的收受报酬的教师，常与道德相对主义、怀疑论、肤浅和不真诚的推理形式联系在一起。

42. **斯巴达**：公元前5世纪的一个希腊城邦，在伯罗奔尼撒战争中击败雅典，成为希腊最重要的城市。

43. **斯多葛学派**：古希腊的一个哲学流派，由基提翁的芝诺在雅典创立。它教导人们，高尚的生活是与自然和谐共处，对痛苦、快乐和财富的短暂性不要太放在心上。

44. **综摄**：不同信仰体系结合或尝试结合成一个新的整体。

45. **神学家**：研究上帝本质和行为的学者。

46. **理念论**：根据柏拉图的理念论，我们能够用感官感知到的一切，都是有关其非物质"理念"的一种形象或印象，即"理念世界"中不变的、必不可少的对应物。柏拉图认为理念是最高的、最基本的一种现实，但如果没有最精细的知识几乎不可能掌握它。

47. **论著**：系统地研究某一特定主题的书面文本（如关于神学或哲学的论著）。

48. **统一论**：一种学术观点，认为柏拉图的哲学教义和信仰在他的所有著作中是一致的。

人名表

1. **阿基琉斯·塔提奥斯**，公元前 2 世纪的希腊作家，除了他的小说《琉基佩和克勒托丰》外，人们对他知之甚少。这部小说在文体方面模仿了柏拉图的《会饮篇》。

2. **阿伽颂**（公元前 448—公元前 400 年），古希腊著名的悲剧作家，也是柏拉图《会饮篇》中的人物。尽管他的戏剧没有一部留存下来，但我们知道，公元前 416 年在会饮发生时，阿伽颂本可以在雅典的莱纳亚音乐节上庆祝他的成功。

3. **米蒂利尼的阿尔凯奥斯**，公元前 6 世纪来自莱斯沃斯岛的希腊抒情诗人。他的诗歌涵盖了多种题材，但最著名的是那些留存下来与政治和对神的赞美有关的不完整的诗歌。

4. **阿尔-法拉比**（870—950），来自突厥斯坦的伊斯兰哲学家。他曾在巴格达学习，广泛游历伊斯兰世界。他的主要哲学著作《优越城居民意见书》透彻而详细地阐述了对柏拉图《理想国》中诸多观点的见解。他的著作对后来的伊斯兰哲学家产生了重要影响。

5. **阿尔西比亚德斯**（公元前 450—公元前 404 年），一位声名狼藉的雅典将军、演说家和政治家，也是柏拉图《会饮篇》中的人物。作为一位才华横溢、个性张扬的军事战略家，他在《会饮篇》写成后不久就被迫逃离雅典，并在被暗杀前向雅典的宿敌斯巴达和波斯告密。

6. **阿普列尤斯**（公元 125—180 年），拉丁语作家和演说家，曾经研究柏拉图哲学。以作品《变形记》闻名，也称《金驴记》。

7. **阿里斯托芬**（约公元前 446—公元前 386 年），一位雅典喜剧作家，柏拉图《会饮篇》中的人物。他有 40 部剧作为人所知，其中有 11 部留存；包括《云》，一部关于哲学和诡辩的戏剧，以一种消极的眼光刻画了苏格拉底。

8. 亚里士多德（公元前384—公元前322年），古希腊哲学家，柏拉图的学生。论著较多，其中最著名的是《尼各马可伦理学》和《形而上学》。他以柏拉图的思想遗产为基础，建立、发展和拓展了自己的哲学。

9. 希波的奥古斯丁（公元354—430年），也称圣奥古斯丁，是一位极具影响力的早期基督教神学家、哲学家和教会主教。他的神学代表作是《忏悔录》和《上帝之城》，其借鉴并发展了柏拉图和新柏拉图思想。

10. 罗兰·巴特（1915—1980），法国重要的文学理论家和哲学家，他围绕结构主义、后结构主义和符号学（符号分析）展开了思想探索。他的作品包括《神话学》和《恋人絮语》，后者大量借鉴了柏拉图的《会饮篇》。

11. 本笃十六世（1927年生，本名若瑟·拉青格），德国籍罗马天主教神学家和牧师。自2005年至2013年，他一直担任罗马天主教的教皇。

12. 莱昂纳多·布鲁尼（1369—1444），意大利人文主义者和历史学家，曾在佛罗伦萨工作。他是研究古代及其所在时代历史的大家，他翻译了柏拉图的《会饮篇》，贡献了一个全新的译本。

13. 雅克·德里达（1930—2004），一位极具影响力的法国大陆哲学家，他发展出一种被称为"解构主义"的符号学分析形式（符号分析）。他的代表作为《论文字学》和《书写与差异》。

14. 恩培多克勒（公元前490—公元前430年），西西里阿克拉噶斯的哲学家。他的代表作《洗心篇》和《论自然》有部分章节留存至今。

15. 厄里什马克（约公元前448年—公元前5世纪末或4世纪初），雅典的医生，在《会饮篇》中出现。

16. 欧里庇得斯（公元前480—公元前406年），古希腊剧作家。他写过90多部戏剧，主要是悲剧，是古雅典文化界最重要的人物之一。

17. 马尔西利奥·费奇诺（1433—1499），意大利文艺复兴早期的重要人物，他将当时已知的柏拉图所有作品译成拉丁文并写了评论。他在著作《论爱》中将《会饮篇》复述了一遍，试图将柏拉图思想与基督教思想结合起来。

18. E.M. 福斯特（1879—1970），英国小说家。他主要以小说《看得见风景的房间》《霍华德庄园》《印度之行》而闻名。

19. 米歇尔·福柯（1926—1984），法国哲学和文化历史学家。他的著作集中于权力与知识理论，其中一部代表作研究性学史，涉及柏拉图的《会饮篇》。

20. 戈特洛布·弗雷格（1848—1925），德国哲学家，以其在逻辑和语言领域对分析哲学的贡献而闻名。他的代表作有《算学基础》。

21. 西格蒙德·弗洛伊德（1856—1939），奥地利精神病学家，公认的"精神分析之父"，其著作中最著名的是《图腾与禁忌》《超越唯乐原则》和《文明及其不满》。

22. 尼撒的贵格利（公元335—394年），一位有影响力的神学家，也是卡帕多西亚早期基督教会的主教。他把柏拉图主义和新柏拉图主义的思想融入到他的神学著作中，如《摩西的生平》。

23. 大卫·霍尔朴林（1952年生），美国性别和性学理论家，著者，密歇根大学研究性史和性理论的杰出教授。他广泛研究了古代和现代的性和性别理论，尤其是柏拉图的爱欲理论。

24. 马丁·海德格尔（1889—1976），德国哲学家，对当代哲学产生了重大影响，以早期著作《存在与时间》闻名。

25. 以弗所的赫拉克利特（约公元前535—公元前475年），哲学家，他的著名理论是万物都处于变化之中。尽管他的著作没有一部留存下来，但我们知道他是《论自然》的作者，该标题被许多早期哲学家使用，他们来自宇宙学、物理学、道德和认识论等领域。

26. 希罗多德（公元前484—公元前425年），来自哈利卡纳索斯的希腊历史学家，以其对历史问题的系统研究而闻名。他的主要著作《历史》详述了希腊和波斯之间的战争。

27. 荷马（约公元前8世纪），古代史诗作者，对古希腊人具有重要意义。他的代表作《伊利亚特》和《奥德赛》对西方思想和文化产生了持久的影响。

28. 索尔·克里普克（1940年生），美国哲学家，普林斯顿大学名誉教授，他的研究集中于数理逻辑、认识论和语言学等领域。其代表作是《命名与必然性》。

29. 雅克·拉康（1901—1981），法国精神分析学家，他的研究建立在弗洛伊德的基础上，其著作作为一系列的研讨材料被出版，其文集《选集》也包含一些关键论文。

30. 虞格仁（1890—1978）是瑞典路德（新教）传统的神学家。他的代表作《圣爱与欲爱》认为，基督教的爱与古希腊的爱欲有着根本的不同。

31. 亚历山大的奥利金（约公元185—253年），有影响力的早期基督教神学家和哲学家。他运用柏拉图和新柏拉图主义思想来思考上帝、开展布道、评论以及撰写《论祈祷》和《论首要原理》。

32. 爱利亚的巴门尼德（公元前6世纪末或5世纪初），哲学家。他的《论自然》是一部形而上学的著作，探讨了可理解的真实的永恒世界和可感知的虚假的变化世界之间的区别。

33. 佩特洛尼乌斯（公元27—66年），罗马帝国时期的一位作家和朝臣。他的作品《萨蒂利孔》戏仿尼禄皇帝奢华的生活方式。

34. 亚历山大的斐洛（公元前20年至公元50年），生活在埃及的犹太哲学家。他的哲学，尤其是在其重要著作《论沉思的生活》中，试图在希腊哲学和犹太哲学的思想之间建立一种综合体。

35. 普罗提诺（公元204—270年），希腊新柏拉图主义哲学家。他的"一、智、魂"三原则的思想，如《九章集》所述，对基督教和文艺复兴思想产生了深远的影响。

36. **普鲁塔克**（公元 46—120 年），希腊历史学家、散文家和传记作家，来自维奥蒂亚。他的著作《爱欲论辩录》受到柏拉图《会饮篇》的影响，也以爱欲为主题。

37. **希拉里·普特南**（1926—2016），分析哲学流派的美国哲学家，著有《逻辑哲学》等，专攻数学、计算机科学和心灵哲学。

38. **彼得·保罗·鲁本斯**（1577—1640），居住在安特卫普的弗拉芒派画家，他的作品具有典型的巴洛克风格。他曾经画过《会饮篇》中的一个场景。

39. **伯特兰·罗素**（1872—1970），英国分析哲学家，以数学家、历史学家和社会评论家的身份而闻名。他最著名的著作是《数学原理》，试图按照逻辑的思路使数学研究系统化。

40. **珀西·比希·雪莱**（1792—1822），著名的英国浪漫主义诗人。他的代表作有经典诗歌《奥兹曼迪亚斯》《阿拉斯特》和《解放了的普罗米修斯》。他也曾翻译过柏拉图的《会饮篇》。

41. **苏格拉底**（公元前 469—公元前 399 年），柏拉图的启蒙老师，古希腊哲学家，柏拉图的《会饮篇》及其他对话录中的核心人物。他没有作品留存。他因使雅典的青少年堕落和自身不虔诚的罪名被判处死刑。

42. **梭伦**（公元前 638—公元前 558 年），雅典的诗人、立法者和政治家。他在公元前 6 世纪末提出了旨在解决雅典城邦道德和政治问题的法案，并被尊为古典时期七贤之一。

43. **麦加拉的泰奥格尼斯**（约公元前 6 世纪），古希腊抒情诗人。其现存的诗歌均以贵族会饮为背景，提出了广泛的实践、政治和道德建议。

44. **格雷戈里·弗拉斯托斯**（1907—1991），研究柏拉图和古典哲学的学者。在《苏格拉底哲学》一书中，弗拉斯托斯为"独特的苏格拉底哲学可以与柏拉图哲学相区分"这一观点辩护。

45. **雅典的色诺芬**（公元前 430—公元前 354 年），古希腊和波斯帝国的哲学家和历史学家。他撰写与苏格拉底相关的著作，探究关于道德、政治生活和家庭管理的问题。

46. **基提翁的芝诺**（公元前334—公元前262年），古希腊哲学家，在雅典建立了斯多葛哲学学派。

WAYS IN TO THE TEXT

KEY POINTS

- Plato was a Greek philosopher of the fifth to the fourth century b.c.e. He is one of the fathers of Western philosophy.
- *Symposium* uses a fictional dialogue to explore the relationship between erotic desire and virtue.
- The text, innovative in both style and philosophy, has influenced thinking about love, desire, and virtue for more than two thousand years.

Who Was Plato?

The Greek philosopher Plato, a disciple of Socrates,* is one of the most famous and influential philosophers in any tradition. Although precise dates are difficult to establish, he is thought to have lived between about 425 and 348 b.c.e. He worked in the Greek city-state of Athens, where he established the philosophical school known as the Academy,* often taken to be the first academic institution of its kind in the Western world. In the period when Plato wrote and taught, Athens was the intellectual and cultural center of the classical world—a hub for philosophical debate and intellectual exchange.

Though some are of doubtful authenticity, Plato is the author of over 30 surviving philosophical dialogues, including *Symposium*, and a number of letters, known as "epistles." The dialogues take the form of philosophical debates between various figures of the day, the philosopher Socrates among them. They address matters such as the life of virtue and what constitutes wisdom (ethics), the ideals of governance and the state (politics), the character of human knowledge and the pursuit of truth (epistemology),* and the fundamental structures of reality (metaphysics).*

After his death, Plato's ideas continued to be discussed at the Academy and other philosophical schools in Athens and subsequently spread across ancient Mediterranean cultures and beyond. Along with his student Aristotle,* Plato laid many of the foundations of Western philosophy and is considered one of the fathers of the Western philosophical tradition. His ideas have been absorbed into the intellectual culture of the West, just as they have influenced thinkers from other cultures, such as medieval Islamic philosophers like Al-Farabi*. They continue to have a great influence today.

What Does *Symposium* Say?

Symposium takes the form of a fictional dialogue between Athens's famous talkers, thinkers, and writers as they discuss matters of love and virtue. The text is structured as a series of speeches at a "symposium," a kind of dinner party at which men of high status would enjoy both material, bodily pleasures (through food, drink, and sex) and the more refined pleasures of the mind (through intellectual discussion). Each of the speeches is framed as being "in praise of Eros"*—the Greek term for the form of love associated with sexual desire and the root of the modern English word "erotic."

The fundamental question that *Symposium* addresses is the role of erotic desire in the philosophical pursuit of wisdom, virtue, and happiness. Specifically, it considers whether Eros is beneficial to the production of philosophy and to the living of an ethical life. Although the text takes the form of an open-ended conversation in which no speech reaches a definite conclusion (which means the dialogue offers many interpretations), we can be safe in understanding that Plato presents erotic desire, as related to philosophy and the virtuous life, in a positive way. This is made especially clear in the words Plato puts in the mouth of his former teacher, Socrates.

Erotic desire for beautiful, material things such as the human body can lead (says Plato's Socrates) to desire and love for higher and more refined forms of beauty such as the beauty of knowledge, virtue, and wisdom. Indeed, Eros should eventually lead us to the contemplation of beauty itself—the final goal of philosophy. The passage describing this journey, referred to as the Ascent to Beauty,* is one of the most famous in the Western tradition. Ultimately, Eros is presented as contributing in crucial ways both to the happiness and well-being of the individual and to the welfare of the community as a whole.

It is no surprise that *Symposium,* having proved to be one of Plato's most influential works, has had a significant impact on later writers and thinkers in two specific respects.

The first is through its literary originality. In describing a fictional dinner party where a philosophical debate is conducted in a light-hearted and often comic fashion, Plato created a type of philosophical literature with many subsequent imitators.[1]

The second is through an analysis of love and erotic desire, and of their relation to virtue and ethics, that has shaped almost every following discussion of any importance on this subject. Plato's student Aristotle, for example, places less emphasis on Eros in his *Nicomachean Ethics*. The difference between Plato's and Aristotle's texts continues to structure many debates around the "ideal" form of love, even in the present day.

Finally, in a broader sense, *Symposium* is of crucial academic and cultural importance as a part of Plato's wider body of work (his corpus), given the general influence of his ideas on the intellectual life of the West, and on philosophy in particular.

Why Does *Symposium* Matter?

Symposium provides an introduction to one of the most influential writers in the history of human thought. In that context alone, its ideas would be worth consideration.

We generally share Plato's assumption that contemplation of *Symposium*'s central themes—love, desire, virtue, wisdom, and happiness—is essential to address the issue of how a life should best be lived. Ancient philosophy is unlike much modern academic philosophy in that it explicitly and continually concerns itself with the question of the "good life;" indeed, in many ways ancient philosophy was understood to be a practice and a way of life in itself.[2] This is evident in *Symposium*, a text concerned with the ways in which desire—and especially erotic desire—can serve virtue and the pursuit of wisdom. Even today, *Symposium* offers us the possibility of reflection on the kinds of lives we might lead, and particularly on how we might think and act in relation to matters of desire and love.

The work's form is also significant. *Symposium*'s complex structure, a long "conversation" in which ideas are never definitively resolved, does not provide the reader with easy answers to the questions it raises. For modern academic writing, this apparent lack of clarity would be regarded as a failing. In Plato's work, however, it is designed to help us realize that the pursuit of wisdom and truth is not necessarily a straightforward task. We cannot always find neat solutions to life's problems.

Symposium tells us that academic study is not simply a question of discovering answers or learning facts. It is about developing ways of thinking and communicating that are valuable in themselves—what Plato would have regarded as intellectual virtues. This is a lesson valuable to students of disciplines beyond philosophy.

Finally, in a more general sense, the influence of Plato, and *Symposium* in particular, onWestern thought and culture is so profound that to study the text is to gain an understanding of the heritage on which modern culture is founded.

---

1. Richard Hunter, *Plato's Symposium* (Oxford: Oxford University Press, 2004), 9–10, 126.
2. Pierre Hadot, *Philosophy as a Way of Life: Spiritual Exercises From Socrates to Foucault,* trans. Michael Chase (Oxford: Wiley-Blackwell, 1995), 49–70, 147–78.

SECTION 1
INFLUENCES

MODULE 1
THE AUTHOR AND THE HISTORICAL CONTEXT

KEY POINTS

- *Symposium* gave rise to a new genre of philosophical literature and has informed debate on the themes of ethics, love, and desire ever since it was written.
- Plato was a student and follower of Socrates,* one of the key characters in *Symposium*.
- In ancient Greece, symposia were social events where both the bodily pleasures of food, drink, and sex and the intellectual pleasures of the mind were enjoyed.

Why Read This Text?

The philosophy of Plato has had an enormous impact on Western thought. But as much as *Symposium* has contributed to that impact, being one of the central texts of Plato's body of work (his corpus), it is also one of his most quirky, challenging, and difficult works.

The text is structured as a fictional dialogue between several of Plato's contemporaries at a "symposium" (a kind of dinner party), where the conversation reaches no definite conclusions. This is perhaps a somewhat complex literary form but one which is highly original in style and which gave rise to a whole new category of philosophical literature.[1]

The text's central themes consider the ways in which erotic desire might contribute positively to the pursuit of virtue and philosophical truth. Plato's reflections on this subject, in speeches given to the characters in the dialogue, have had an important influence on Western thought, from the classical philosophers of his own era such as his student Aristotle,* to some of the most important Christian* theologians (those who study God) like St. Augustine.* This influence continues to be felt in the work of modern scholars in a wide variety of fields. Alongside Plato's discussions of similar subjects in his *Lysis* and *Phaedrus*, *Symposium* continues to be studied because of its literary originality, its philosophical merit, and its cultural impact across many centuries.

> "Both the setting of this dialogue at a symposium, and the focus on the erotic relationships that typically took place at such an event, is a natural way in which to explore the ethics of desire in [ancient Greek] culture, since the context itself was one which attempted to make Eros* work towards certain cultural norms."
>
> ——Frisbee C. C. Sheffield, *Plato's Symposium: The Ethics of Desire*

Author's Life

The philosopher Plato is thought to have been born in or near Athens around 425 B.C.E. to parents with illustrious ancestors. His father, Ariston, was related to a former king of Athens, while the family of his mother, Perictione, was linked to Solon,* an important Athenian lawgiver of the late sixth century B.C.E.[2] Plato grew up in Athens, a city where thinkers, poets, and philosophers congregated.

His education was typical of an elite Athenian male. He learned letters (formal scholarship and literature) and wrestling in private schools before taking up creative activities such as painting and the composition of poetry, especially tragedies.[3]

In his youth Plato spent time talking and discussing with philosophers. It is recorded that he was influenced by a thinker who knew and understood the ideas of Heraclitus,* an older philosopher who believed that the nature and structure of the world was maintained through the dynamic action of change.[4] When he later encountered the philosopher Socrates, Plato quickly became a follower. Socrates remained the most important influence on Plato's life and philosophy, and features as one of the key characters in *Symposium*.

Like most Athenians, Plato followed a polytheistic* religion. This meant he believed in the existence of several gods and goddesses. Religious rituals were a part of both political and social life to the extent that modern scholars find it difficult to distinguish between religious identity and civic identity* in ancient Athens. In particular, it is worth bearing in mind Plato's exposure to mystery cults, in which political and religious forms of identity were intertwined, since revelation was reserved for a select group of initiates. The Eleusinian Mysteries* that took place near Athens, for example, provide a backdrop to *Symposium*'s presentation of the ritual ascent to the Form of Beauty.*[5] The philosopher is here depicted as progressing from desire for material things, such as beautiful bodies, to immaterial things, such as beautiful ideas, finally to a contemplation of beauty itself, in its eternal and unchanging form, beyond matter and time.

Author's Background

It is likely that Plato wrote *Symposium* in Athens, the main intellectual center of the ancient Greek world. Described as "the enlightened city *par excellence*,"⁶ it was a place of great commercial, institutional, poetical, and philosophical energy where ideas were generated and presented to eager audiences in theaters, courtrooms, public assemblies, and in philosophical debates. Having founded his philosophical school, the Academy,* in Athens, Plato went on to contribute to the intellectually fertile environment that had made him.

The title of Plato's *Symposium* refers to the work's fictional setting: an all-male social gathering with drinking, dining, intellectual conversation, and other forms of entertainment that usually included paid performers, both musical and sexual. Throughout the ancient Greek world, a symposium was an event for men of high status. As an occasion where cultural values and ideas were enacted and transmitted from one generation to another, it represented more than a mere dinner party.⁷ It stood, in effect, for an aristocratic "alternative society"⁸ operating in parallel to the more democratic and open institutions of the Athenian city-state of the fifth century b.c.e. The title, therefore, does not merely name the setting for Plato's philosophical treatise,* it indicates the intellectual and cultural framework in which the work is positioned.

Although *Symposium* was written in approximately 380

B.C.E.,[9] it describes a fictional symposium held in 416 B.C.E. (that is, more than 30 years earlier). The "cast" includes several of the period's most important figures—the philosopher Socrates, the playwrights Aristophanes* and Agathon,* and the infamous young general Alcibiades,* whose actions after 416 B.C.E. played a pivotal role in the outcome of the Peloponnesian War* between Athens and Sparta.*[10]

From the perspective of the audience in 380 B.C.E., *Symposium* does not simply consider timeless philosophical questions about virtue and desire. It puts them in the mouths of historical characters who were of significance to the people of the day. It is especially worth noting the context provided by the execution of one of *Symposium*'s main characters, Socrates, in 399 B.C.E. Socrates had a hold on the Athenian imagination, and was an important figure in Plato's own life. The vivid picture *Symposium* paints of him would surely have made people think, if only implicitly, about the charges of which he was convicted: namely, corrupting the youth of Athens and impiety towards the gods of the state.[11]

---

1. Richard Hunter, *Plato's Symposium* (Oxford: Oxford University Press, 2004), 9–10, 126.
2. W. K. C. Guthrie, *A History of Greek Philosophy,* vol. 4, *Plato: The Man and His Dialogues: Earlier Period* (Cambridge: Cambridge University Press, 1986), 10.
3. Guthrie, *History of Greek Philosophy,* vol. 4, 12–7.
4. Guthrie, *History of Greek Philosophy,* vol. 4, 33; Debra Nails, *The People of Plato: A Prosopography of Plato and Other Socratics* (Indianapolis: Hackett Publishing, 2002), 105–6.
5. Frisbee C. C. Sheffield, *Plato's Symposium: The Ethics of Desire* (Oxford: Oxford University Press, 2006), 219.

6. Steven Berg, *Eros and the Intoxications of Enlightenment: On Plato's Symposium* (Albany, NY: State University of New York Press, 2010), x.
7. Hunter, *Plato's Symposium*, 5–7.
8. Hunter, *Plato's Symposium*, 6.
9. K. Dover, "The Date of Plato's *Symposium*," *Phronesis* 10 (1965): 2–20; Hunter, *Plato's Symposium*, 3.
10. Hunter, *Plato's Symposium*, 4–5.
11. Berg, *Eros and the Intoxications of Enlightenment*, x–xii.

MODULE 2
ACADEMIC CONTEXT

KEY POINTS
- Ancient Greek philosophy is concerned with fundamental questions about the nature of reality and the character of a good human life.
- At the time of *Symposium*'s writing, Eros* (that is, the influence of love and sexual desire) was not considered fundamentally related to philosophy or the pursuit of the "good life."
- Plato questions commonly held views of the time by celebrating erotic desire as fundamental for philosophy and the virtuous life.

The Work in Its Context

In ancient Greece, the student of philosophy—a word that literally means "love of wisdom," from the Greek words *philia* and *sophos*—was someone engaged in the study of the fundamental structures of reality and the nature of the good and virtuous life. This included the school of Pythagoreanism,* which sought to describe the world as a coherent mathematical system. According to tradition, Plato is said to have spent time with Pythagorean philosophers in southern Italy.[1]

Earlier philosophers such as Parmenides* and Heraclitus* also influenced Plato. Parmenides described the theory that our sensory faculties prevent us from recognizing the unified, unchangeable, and timeless nature of existence.[2] The theory implied a criticism of Heraclitus, who held that the cosmos existed in a state of perpetual flux.[3] Socrates,* however, was the strongest direct influence on Plato.

For Athenian citizens of Plato's time, "the nature of virtue" was well established as a subject for debate, both inside and outside of symposium.[4] The concept of Eros was generally seen as an equivocal*—ambiguous—external force that needed regulating.[5] Eros could be portrayed as making characters act against their will in the tragedies of dramatic theatre, or used to conceptualize the irrational behavior of the citizens' assembly when swayed by the speech of a politician.[6]

> "In both its form and its content ... The Symposium is intimately related to Plato's larger ethical concerns with the nature of the good life. Erotic relationships, of the sort that all the speakers are concerned with, and which typically took place at symposia, were an important way in which virtue was transmitted."
>
> —— Frisbee C. C. Sheffield, *Plato's Symposium: The Ethics of Desire*

Overview of the Field

It is worth considering what Plato thought and wrote about the sophists,* a section of the intellectual class who taught rhetoric* (how to talk and discuss effectively) and the arts of disputation* (arguing and debating) for financial reward. The sophists, of whom Plato asserts in his *Protagoras* that they believed they could teach virtue, were enticing to their audiences. But conservative sections of society disapproved of them. Plato criticized them rigorously throughout his work, saying they were only really interested in money and hedonism* (the pursuit of pleasure) and thus posed a risk to the souls of their impressionable students.

For Plato, philosophy was both a form of education and a practice to be lived. He believed it should be taught for free, and the sophists were incapable of embodying this virtue, one of the discipline's main aims.[7] Plato was greatly troubled by the damaging effects on education of the forms of rhetoric taught by the sophists. His inquiry into the use of Eros in philosophy should be considered against the background of these anxieties.

The influence on Plato's thinking of ancient Greece's literary traditions should also be noted. The epic poems* attributed to Homer* shaped Greek notions of morality generally, while the comic and tragic playwrights active in the Athens of the fifth century b.c.e. influenced Plato's thinking more specifically. Indeed, *Symposium* features characters who were themselves playwrights, and adapts motifs, images, and ideas that had been explored in the theater (notably that of the irresistible power and effects of Eros). In Greek literature, Eros had generally been presented as an irresistible external force that could drive an individual to act against their better judgment or good advice.[8] Plato's more positive depiction of Eros must be considered in this light.

Academic Influences

Aristotle records that Plato's first philosophical experience came from the Heraclitean* philosopher Cratylus, with whom Plato associated as a young man.[9] While Plato incorporated certain of Heraclitus's ideas into his thought, he rejected his central theory that everything was in a state of flux, or more precisely, that the stability of the whole was only achieved through constant alteration. In distinction, Plato's metaphysics would go on to contrast this Heraclitean world of perceptible change with a prior and more perfect world of unchanging forms, whose intellectual apprehension held the key to true knowledge and virtue.[10]

Undoubtedly the most important direct influence on Plato was his teacher Socrates, to whom Plato gives a central role in *Symposium*. However, it is difficult for scholars to distinguish the views of Socrates himself from those of Plato[11] because we have no firsthand record of Socrates' own beliefs. The establishment of clear lines of influence from one to the other is at the root of what is known as the "Socratic Problem," an issue that has been with us so long that it has been described as "insoluble."[12]

Through its response to the debate of the time about the relationship between erotic desire and philosophy, *Symposium* fundamentally altered the shape of that discussion. In the dialogue's longest speech, that of Socrates, Plato reinterprets Eros as an internal force capable of motivating philosophical reflection and the pursuit of virtue.[13] In this way he questions the prevailing view of Eros as an invasive force that provokes irrational behavior.

Plato achieves his purpose by giving an account of a fictional symposium. While this was not an entirely new literary device in itself, his was the first piece of work to portray a symposium in order to conduct a philosophical exploration of ethics and desire. As a result we can say that the book's seminal nature is derived from the combination of its literary form and its philosophical content.

Symposium did not emerge from a vacuum, as an act of pure originality, but drew from the literary, philosohical, and social environment of the period's culture. Plato's innovation lies in his bringing unfamiliar ideas and categories into conversation with one another to create something radically new.

---

1. W. K. C. Guthrie, *A History of Greek Philosophy,* vol. 4, *Plato: The Man and His Dialogues: Earlier Period* (Cambridge: Cambridge University Press, 1986), 35–6.
2. Guthrie, *History of Greek Philosophy,* vol. 4, 34–5.
3. Guthrie, *History of Greek Philosophy,* vol. 4, 33.
4. Frisbee C. C. Sheffield, *Plato's Symposium: The Ethics of Desire* (Oxford: Oxford University Press, 2006), 4–5.
5. Sheffield, *Plato's Symposium*, 5.
6. Richard Hunter, *Plato's Symposium* (Oxford: Oxford University Press, 2004), 16–8.
7. Marina McCoy, *Plato on the Rhetoric of Philosophers and Sophists* (Cambridge: Cambridge University Press, 2011), 1–3.
8. Hunter, *Plato's Symposium*, 17.
9. Debra Nails, *The People of Plato: A Prosopography of Plato and Other Socratics* (Indianapolis: Hackett Publishing, 2002), 105–6.
10. Guthrie, *History of Greek Philosophy,* vol. 4, 33.
11. William Prior, "Socrates (historical)," in *The Continuum Companion to Plato*, ed. Gerald A. Press (London: Continuum, 2012), 29–30.
12. Prior, "Socrates (historical)," 29.
13. Plato, *The Symposium* in Plato: The Symposium, trans. M. C. Howatson, ed. M. C. Howatson and Frisbee C. C. Sheffield (Cambridge: Cambridge University Press, 2008), 32–50.

MODULE 3
THE PROBLEM

KEY POINTS

- *Symposium* looks to answer two key questions. What is the true nature of Eros?* And what is its relation to the philosophical pursuit of truth and virtue?
- Eros was generally thought of as an intrusive and unknowable external force, often going against reason.
- Plato moves beyond the generally held view by suggesting that erotic desire *can* provide a basis for the pursuit of virtue and wisdom and a true understanding of beauty.

Core Question

The overall core question that Plato's *Symposium* addresses is whether or not Eros has any place in the pursuit of philosophy. Plato finds that it does and suggests it is important for the ethical well-being of the individual and also for the cohesion of the community. To understand the particular importance given to Eros in *Symposium*, it is necessary to consider Plato's specific understanding of the cultural context in which he worked.

The text's inquiry takes place in a fictional symposium—a culturally significant social occasion attended by ancient Athens's men of high status.[1] One important aspect of the ancient symposium was its role as a venue for the practice of pederasty,* an arrangement between men of different ages according to which the junior partner was instructed in virtue and knowledge by the elder.[2]

In these relationships, of course, erotic desire for the body of another was central. Although these arrangements were scrutinized and often liable to charges of corruption, *Symposium* explores the ways in which such relationships might demonstrate, develop, or serve as a foundation for different aspects of virtue and wisdom. This is especially true of the long speech that Plato gives to Socrates.*

> *"As Eros is [traditionally] an invasive force from outside, its presence can be shaming and disorienting, in that it takes away one's better judgment and one's sense of independence; Eros forces us to confront our lack and need, ideas which are to be fundamental to* Symposium.*"*
>
> ——Richard Hunter, *Plato*'s *Symposium*

The Participants

Eros had previously been depicted in Greek literature as an important physical principle that allowed mortal beings to reproduce and also drove the fertility of their natural environment. Eros was said to make itself felt through a desire similar to the desire the rain feels for the ground.[3]

In general, "Eros in archaic poetry may, in the broadest terms, be thought of as an invasive force or emotion which drives one to wish to satisfy a felt need."[4] This "invasive force" was often presented as an ambiguous power that overwhelmed its subject and caused individuals to act irrationally in pursuit of their desire. As this invasion was typically framed as an act of the gods, Eros was also seen as a kind of divine power. In Euripides'* plays *Medea* and *Hippolytus*, for example, the characters of Medea and Phaedra both experience this uncontrollable force.[5] It is associated with an overwhelming feeling of a lack of what they desire and an equally irresistible urge to fill that lack.

It was this conception of Eros that formed the intellectual and cultural background to Plato's own discussion of the subject in *Symposium*.

The Contemporary Debate

By considering the possibility that, rather than being an unmanageable external influence, Eros might be both generated internally and might lead to the attainment and maintenance of virtue, Plato goes against the dominant views of his time.

Although he argues against the prevailing view, notably in the speech he gives to Socrates,[6] Plato does not directly engage with those writers and thinkers who present contrary interpretations of Eros. As a work produced in the context of the wider intellectual currents of ancient Athens, *Symposium*'s presentation of Eros would have been remarkable enough in its own right. But what is more, such a direct engagement would not have been appropriate to the literary form Plato chose for his work, which is a dialogue between several speakers.

Plato has each speaker compete in giving an *encomium*—that is, a speech of praise—on the subject of Eros. While this blurs the boundary between the serious and the comic, and sees Plato engaging in both artistic parody and abstract philosophical argument, Eros is described throughout in positive terms. By associating erotic desire with lack (especially in the speech given to Aristophanes,* who defines it as "the desire and pursuit of the whole"),[7] Plato highlights an idea that would certainly have been familiar to his peers. Similarly, the idea that Eros is associated with a lack of reason is represented in *Symposium* by the speech Plato gives to Alcibiades,* who describes philosophy as a "madness and frenzy" caused by the venomous bite of Eros to the "heart or soul."[8]

The polyphonic* nature of the text—that is, the inclusion of several voices—and the fact that it is presented as a secondhand (reported) account, makes it difficult to perfectly define its philosophical argument. Nevertheless, the sixth speech, the one given to Socrates, has generally been seen to offer *Symposium*'s central conclusion, given that the ideas it describes overlap with central ideas Plato portrays elsewhere in his body of work.

---

1. Richard Hunter, *Plato's Symposium* (Oxford: Oxford University Press, 2004), 5–7.
2. Hunter, *Plato's Symposium,* 5–7; Frisbee C. C. Sheffield, "Introduction," Plato: The Symposium, trans. M. C. Howatson, eds. M. C. Howatson and Frisbee C. C. Sheffield (Cambridge: Cambridge University Press, 2008), viii–x.
3. Hunter, *Plato's Symposium*, 17.
4. Hunter, *Plato's Symposium*, 16.
5. Hunter, *Plato's Symposium*, 17–8.
6. Plato, *The Symposium*, in Plato: The Symposium trans. M. C. Howatson, ed. M. C. Howatson and Frisbee C. C. Sheffield (Cambridge: Cambridge University Press, 2008), 32–50.
7. Plato, *The Symposium*, 26.
8. Plato, *The Symposium*, 57.

MODULE 4
THE AUTHOR'S CONTRIBUTION

KEY POINTS

* Erotic desire can lead the philosopher to the sight of the very Form of Beauty* itself, from which comes true virtue.
* *Symposium* makes original arguments about Eros's* positive contribution both to the virtuous life and the nature of beauty. In writing it, Plato created a new form of philosophical literature.
* In ancient Greece, symposia provided a place for erotic practices, education, instruction, and ethical debate and conversation. Plato makes use of this connection for his own philosophical ends.

Author's Aims

In *Symposium*, Plato's chief aim is to discuss the relationship between Eros and ethics, happiness, truth, and education. In doing so, Plato moves away from the philosophical inquiries of his contemporaries by conjoining the realms of morality, ethics, and Eros. He does this through an elaborate literary construction in which key ideas are skilfully embedded in a narrative (in this instance, a fictional dialogue taking place at a symposium).

Symposia had previously been used as settings for thinking about ethics by poets of the sixth century b.c.e. such as Theognis of Megara* and Alcaeus of Mytilene.* The historian Herodotus* (fifth century b.c.e.) described them in a celebrated book on the history and peoples of the Mediterranean region.[1] It is Plato's account, however, with its depth of philosophical ideas and its depiction of wise men at intellectual play, that is considered to be the source of viewing the symposium as a learned dinner party where philosophy is served in an entertaining fashion.[2]

The themes of the text emerge from the speeches given by each of the seven characters at symposium. Plato's structuring of this fictional event is designed to allow the speeches to enrich and complement, critique and modify, restate and undercut the ideas and themes that arise.

Socrates' speech, the sixth, being the longest and the most philosophically rich, is said to embody the central themes of the work and to resolve the questions raised by the other speeches.[3] Here Plato explores the original idea that erotic desire can provide a positive and fruitful foundation for the philosophical pursuit of wisdom and virtue when that desire is acted upon "correctly."

> *"The correct way for him to go ... to the things of love, is to begin from the beautiful things of the world, and using these as steps, to climb ever upwards for the sake of that other beauty, going from one to two and from two to all beautiful bodies, and from beautiful bodies to beautiful practices, and beautiful practices to beautiful kinds of knowledge, and from beautiful kinds of knowledge finally to that particular beauty which is knowledge solely of the beautiful itself, so that at last he may know what the beautiful really is."*
>
> —— Plato, Socrates'* speech in *Symposium*

Approach

Each of the seven speakers in *Symposium* delivers a speech in praise of Eros. While each one is important for an understanding of the text as a whole, the speech Plato gives to Socrates offers the most surprising investigation of Plato's core question. It is notably inventive in its suggestion that the erotic desire for beauty is capable of making a positive contribution to the philosophical pursuit of virtue and wisdom.

This is detailed most famously in the passage concerning the Ascent to Beauty,* according to which the person who has allowed Eros to take hold progresses from the experience of beautiful bodies to the love of beautiful souls, and from there to the appreciation of beauty in laws and institutions and branches of knowledge. The final step is the sight and understanding of the Form of Beauty, something that exists outside the changing world of appearances.[4]

The key point that Plato's Socrates makes in his speech is that when erotic desire for what is beautiful is pursued in the right way and in the right order, it will be beneficial to the acquisition of virtue and wisdom. In this sense, erotic desire is seen as positively related to reason and philosophy, rather than a hindrance.

Although it is intended to be a significant speech, the literary construction of the whole text with its multiple narrators prevents us from forming firm conclusions based on Socrates' words alone. Indeed, after he has finished speaking, the whole dynamic of *Symposium* changes when the boisterous politician Alcibiades* intrudes with a crowd of partygoers and alters the mood with a rather drunken speech in praise of Socrates himself.⁵ Plato uses the discourse of Alcibiades to highlight the difficulty of analyzing Socrates and uncovering the truth and wisdom in his words.⁶ The speech tells us that "reading this or any work of Plato requires effort and thought, requires us in fact to 'get inside' Socrates' words."⁷ Mingling the literary with the philosophical in this way, Plato's approach in *Symposium* is both innovative and appealing for the reader.

Contribution in Context

By considering the possibility that Eros might be an internal force conducive to the flourishing of virtue, Plato resists the commonly held views of his time.

A symposium provided a setting where erotic activities took place alongside education and instruction.*⁸ For Plato to frame his philosophical exploration as a dialogue taking place at one of these events was innovative.

Despite using a literary form considered out of the ordinary in its day, the work nevertheless draws on the ideas of earlier philosophers. For example, *Symposium*'s inquiry into the role and importance of Eros is borrowed from Empedocles,* a philosopher of the mid fifth century b.c.e., most notably in the speeches Plato gives to Aristophanes* and Eryximachus.*⁹ Empedocles presents a vision of the natural evolution and alteration of the universe as being driven by the competing forces of strife and love—although he uses the Greek word *philia* (love or friendship) rather than Plato's more intense Eros (the force of love or desire). Plato's exploration of Eros translates Empedocles' cosmic force into an internal source of power capable of uniting individuals with those they love, while offering the possibility of limitless virtue.

In the speech Plato gives to Socrates, beauty is described as abstract and unchanging. Contemplation of beauty, Socrates tells us, generates true wisdom. This is an idea adapted from Parmenides of Elea,* a philosopher of the early fifth century b.c.e. who believed that the sensible world (that is, the world we can perceive with our senses) was a deceptive version of a true, unchanging, and eternal reality in the form of a perfect sphere. Plato's Theory of Forms* and their role in the attainment of knowledge owes something to this idea. In *Symposium* we read that the practice of philosophy allows us to transcend the material world and attain the realm of abstract beauty. Plato differs from Parmenides in his belief that Eros has a role to play in the education needed to ascend to a glimpse of the ideal Form of Beauty.

---

1. Richard Hunter, *Plato's Symposium* (Oxford: Oxford University Press, 2004), 14–5.
2. Hunter, *Plato's Symposium,* 9–10, 126.
3. Plato, *The Symposium*, in Plato: The Symposium, trans. M. C. Howatson, ed. M. C. Howatson and Frisbee C. C. Sheffield (Cambridge: Cambridge University Press, 2008), 32–50.
4. Plato, *The Symposium*, 48–9.
5. Plato, *The Symposium*, 51–63.
6. Plato, *The Symposium*, 55–7.

7. Hunter, *Plato's Symposium*, 11.
8. Hunter, *Plato's Symposium*, 5–7; Frisbee C. C. Sheffield, "Introduction," Plato: The Symposium, trans. M. C. Howatson, eds. M. C. Howatson and Frisbee C. C. Sheffield (Cambridge: Cambridge University Press, 2008), viii–x.
9. Catherine H. Zuckert, *Plato's Philosophers: The Coherence of the Dialogues* (Chicago: University of Chicago Press, 2009), 289–90.

SECTION 2
IDEAS

MODULE 5
MAIN IDEAS

KEY POINTS

- *Symposium* explores the nature of Eros* and its relation to philosophical and ethical life.
- Erotic desire, pursued in the right manner and sequence, can generate virtue and wisdom.
- The text is a series of speeches at a specific kind of social event. Every speech in praise of Eros qualifies the other.

Key Themes

In Plato's *Symposium* we follow a fictional debate on the nature of erotic love—Eros—and its relation to wisdom and the ethical life.

Asked "to make a speech in praise of Love,"[1] each participant at a symposium presents an alternative definition of Eros, incorporating ideas taken from myth, literature, medicine, history, and philosophy. Through this dialogue, the text discusses key ethical, social and educational themes: how to teach wisdom; how to instil a sense of respect and bravery; how to maintain physical, emotional and spiritual health; how inspiration and excellence emerge; how one might attain wisdom, truth and happiness through the contemplation of beauty.

The central speech, given by Plato to Socrates,* seeks to explain the ways in which erotic desire can provide a foundation for the philosophical pursuit of truth and virtue—assuming that the desire is acted upon correctly.

The form in which these ideas are presented (a series of speeches by men at a social event) also allows *Symposium* to address themes such as the nature of male friendship, and to provide a commentary on the effects of rhetoric* on truth—a concern that runs through much of Plato's work.[2]

> *"Anyone who has been guided to this point in the study of love and has been contemplating beautiful things in the correct way and in the right sequence, will suddenly perceive, as he now approaches the end of his study, a beauty that is marvellous in its nature—the very thing ... for the sake of which all the earlier labors were undertaken."*
>
> —— Plato, Socrates' speech in *Symposium*

Exploring the Ideas

The clearest outline of Plato's key ideas is presented in the words he puts into the mouth of Socrates.

Socrates declares that the speeches that have been made before his have glorified the speaker rather than the nature of Eros.[3] Those speeches, he says, praised the quality of those who are loved, rather than Eros itself as it moves the lover. For Socrates, erotic love is defined as a compulsive striving after what is most beautiful. And what is most beautiful must be that which is most good: "The fact is that the only thing people love is the good."[4]

However, this pursuit does not end with possession of "the good." Its object is to generate "wisdom and the rest of virtue ... the good ordering of cities and households ... moderation and justice."[5]

In other words, as a pursuit of what is beautiful and good, Eros is firmly associated with the philosophical life as a practice in its own right. And the aim of this practice is virtue.

Socrates' analysis culminates in a celebrated passage describing the Ascent to Beauty.*6 In this section, the one who seeks virtue and truth advances from the appreciation of beauty in material things, such as the human body, to the appreciation of things that are not material, such as beautiful souls and forms of knowledge. The final aim is to see and understand the unchanging Form of Beauty* itself. While everything worthy of contemplation has something of beauty in it, the Form of Beauty itself is eternal and unalterable:"It does not come into being or waste away ... It exists on its own, single in substance and everlasting."7 Erotic desire, if acted upon mindfully (says Socrates), can take us to this level.

Language and Expression

Symposium's main themes emerge from the seven speeches given in the course of the symposium Plato describes. The work is structured to allow the various descriptions of the nature and function of Eros to qualify and enrich one another. As a consequence, we are obliged to consider the text's philosophical ideas and the way those ideas are presented together.

Plato, it seems, was aware of this. He claimed throughout the body of his work that the rhetorical practices of his period were concerned with the persuasion and enchantment of one's audience, rather than with the truth. In what is arguably a self-referential comment, Socrates begins his speech by accusing those who spoke before him of praising themselves rather than Eros, commenting sarcastically that it "seems that the original proposal was not that each should really praise Love but that we should give the appearance of doing so."[8] If rhetoric's purpose is persuasion (as Plato seems to acknowledge), it does not automatically make a "successful" argument true—and it has nothing to do with the purity of the arguer's intentions, either.

It is worth noting that *Symposium*'s inquiry into knowledge reaches no definite conclusion. It does not end when Socrates has finished speaking, but when the others present fall asleep.[9]

The text may be difficult to interpret definitively but this is not a shortcoming. It is central to Plato's intention to encourage the reader to continue in the pursuit of wisdom, questioning previous judgements and reassessing the basis of any claim to knowledge. In this sense *Symposium* does not present a closed doctrine for the reader to memorize, but a series of challenges and ideas useful for the practice of philosophy.

Plato's description of the Ascent to Beauty has proved to be one of the most striking images in Western literature and philosophy; indeed, it has been said that it has done "much to mold the European imagination."[10] It brilliantly encapsulates his view of the purpose of philosophical activity and its role in education.

Although the final significance of *Symposium* in the context of Plato's thought as a whole remains open to interpretation, it is true that it transforms the discipline of "philosophy"—that is, the *philia* ("friendly" love) of *sophos* (wisdom)—to an "erotic" (that is, loving and self-perpetuating) desire for wisdom.

1. Plato, *The Symposium*, in Plato: The Symposium, trans. M. C. Howatson, ed. M. C. Howatson and Frisbee C. C. Sheffield (Cambridge: Cambridge University Press, 2008), 7.
2. Marina McCoy, *Plato on the Rhetoric of Philosophers and Sophists* (Cambridge: Cambridge University Press, 2011), 1–3.
3. Plato, *The Symposium*, 33.
4. Plato, *The Symposium*, 43.
5. Plato, *The Symposium*, 47.
6. Plato, *The Symposium*, 48–9.
7. Plato, *The Symposium*, 49.
8. Plato, *The Symposium*, 32–3.
9. Plato, *The Symposium*, 63.
10. Gregory Vlastos. "The Individual as an Object of Love in Plato," in *Platonic Studies,* ed. Gregory Vlastos (Princeton NJ: Princeton University Press, 1973), 24.

MODULE 6
SECONDARY IDEAS

KEY POINTS

* The speech of Aristophanes* presents an original myth of erotic desire resulting from a primordial lack.
* Aristophanes' speech has been interpreted as conveying an original theory of gender and sexual desire. Its concerns are somewhat different to those of the central speech given to Socrates.*
* The philosophical merit of the speech given to Eryximachus* has often been overlooked.

Other Ideas

The subject of every speech in Plato's *Symposium* is Eros* (the force of desire, often associated with sexual love) and its relation to friendship, ethics and education. Although these reflections reach a culmination in the major discourse of Plato's teacher Socrates, the speeches given to the playwright Aristophanes and the statesman Alcibiades* are also worth noting. Aristophanes and Alcibiades express their ideas by referencing dramatic myth in vivid characterization, and in compelling depictions of both the debilitating and the healing powers of Eros.

The speech given to Aristophanes paints a picture of the origin of the human race through a mythology unique to Plato in which erotic desire has its origin in a very ancient lack.[1] The concluding speech Plato gives to Alcibiades, meanwhile, explores Eros's physical dimensions and its relation to the "madness" of philosophy.

> *"Each of us is a mere tally of a person, one of two sides of a filleted fish, one half of an original whole. We are continually searching for our other half."*
>
> —— Plato, the speech of Aristophanes in *Symposium*

Exploring the Ideas

Aristophanes' mythological depiction of the origin of the human race is unique to Plato, and one of his most interesting innovations.[2] The speech claims that the current mortal condition of the human race is a degraded state; that we were originally spherical and double (paired one of three ways: male—female, female—female, or male—male) and that Zeus cut us in half as a punishment. Now separated from our other halves, we humans are compelled to search for the part that completes us. It is this original pairing (according to Plato's Aristophanes) that determines the object of our erotic desires.

As a consequence, Eros is portrayed as a healer capable of bringing mortals back to happiness and wholeness and whose role "is to restore our ancient state by trying to make unity out of duality and to heal our human condition."[3] Desire, in other words, has its origin in an ancient lack, and an individual who doesn't resolve this deficiency is consigned to a state of depression and lethargy. This idea is contrary to the Greek consensus on sexual categories and gender.[4]

Being less focused on the relationship between Eros, education and virtue, such a depiction of Eros is distinct from other ideas in *Symposium*. It offers a startling vision of Eros and the challenge of emotional fulfillment that has fascinated subsequent generations of readers.[5]

The speech of Alcibiades, like that of Socrates, discusses the role of Eros in the formation of true virtue and in the philosopher's Ascent to Beauty.* Coming at the end of *Symposium*, the speech pulls the reader back from the abstract intellectualism of Socrates to the physical and emotional desires of individuals.[6] Alcibiades' characterization of philosophy as a "madness and frenzy" caused by the venomous bite of Eros to the "heart or soul"[7] differs from Socrates' more harmonious account of the erotic Ascent to Beauty, and is more in keeping with the dominant contemporary view of Eros as an invasive, destabilizing force.

After receiving such a bite, Alcibiades says, "there is nothing [a man] will not do or say."[8] Plato's decision to present these ideas by means of the historical person of Alcibiades—a controversial politician and general who was assassinated—leaves questions about the complex connections between philosophy, Eros and political life (an underlying theme of the text).[9] The speech also highlights the challenges of interpretation that *Symposium* presents for its readers. It compares Socrates and his discourses to a statue of the god Silenus* which contains smaller, more beautiful, statues within it. "I don't know if anyone else has seen the statues he has inside, but I saw them once, and they seemed to me divine and golden, so utterly beautiful and wonderful."[10]

This is a both a warning against trusting in surface appearances and an indication that the true marvels of virtue may be concealed. This is an important point to remember in interpreting the words of

Socrates' and the other speakers.[11]

Overlooked

According to the traditional interpretation, we should look to the speeches of Alcibiades, Aristophanes, and Socrates for Plato's most important metaphysical* ideas. (Metaphysics is the study of the fundamental structures of reality.) However, the speech given to the doctor Eryximachus has perhaps been overlooked, often being regarded as "much less generally accessible" and "taken to be just a parody of the jargon-ridden 'grand unifying theories' of fifth-century science and medicine."[12]

Eryximachus attempts to explain the unity of the arts and sciences in terms of "good" and "bad" kinds of love, taking various disciplines in turn to explain his point.[13] "I shall start by speaking about medicine, in order to give pride of place to that profession,"[14] he announces in a discourse often regarded as self-serving and weighted towards his own preferences[15] (notably perhaps in his somewhat patronizing use of the philosophy of Heraclitus*).[16] Eryximachus's excessive concern with minor details has led some readers to argue that Plato is more interested in caricaturing an intellectual type than in a precise exploration of ideas. As a result, the speech has been dismissed as having little philosophical merit. Yet the idea that Eryximachus does not take himself as seriously as it seems at first has begun to yield insights into how his speech contributes positively to *Symposium*. There remains room for further research of this issue.[17]

1. Plato, *The Symposium*, in Plato: The Symposium, trans. M. C. Howatson, ed. M. C. Howatson and Frisbee C. C. Sheffield (Cambridge: Cambridge University Press, 2008), 22–7.
2. Plato, *The Symposium*, 22–7.
3. Plato, *The Symposium*, 24.
4. Jeffrey Carnes, "The Myth Which is Not One: Construction of Discourse in Plato's Symposium," in *Rethinking Sexuality: Foucault and Classical Antiquity*, ed. David H. J. Larmour et al. (Princeton, NJ: Princeton University Press, 1998), 105.
5. Richard Hunter, *Plato's Symposium* (Oxford: Oxford University Press, 2004), 68–9.
6. Plato, *The Symposium*, 51–63.
7. Plato, *The Symposium*, 57.
8. Plato, *The Symposium*, 57.
9. Cf. Steven Berg, *Eros and the Intoxications of Enlightenment: On Plato's Symposium* (Albany, NY: State University of New York Press, 2010), x–xii, 131–50.
10. Plato, *The Symposium*, 56.
11. Deborah Tarn Steiner, *Images in Mind: Statues in Archaic and Classical Greek Literature and Thought* (Princeton, NJ: Princeton University Press, 2002), 89.
12. Hunter, *Plato's Symposium*, 54.
13. Plato, *The Symposium*, 18–22.
14. Plato, *The Symposium*, 18.
15. Kevin Corrigan and Elena Glazov-Corrigan, *Plato's Dialectic at Play: Argument, Structure, and Myth in Symposium* (University Park, PA: The Pennsylvania State University Press, 2004), 63.
16. Plato, *Symposium*, 19; Corrigan and Glazov-Corrigan, *Plato's Dialectic at Play*, 63–5.
17. Hunter, *Plato's Symposium*, 53–9.

MODULE 7
ACHIEVEMENT

KEY POINTS
- Plato's exploration of love, desire, beauty, and virtue in *Symposium* has had an immense influence on Western thought from antiquity* (the period before the Middle Ages) to the present day.
- The text's originality, both in terms of its literary form and its philosophical argument, has guaranteed its continuing importance.
- Christian* mystical* interpretations of the text have sometimes obscured its emphasis on physical sexual desire.

Assessing the Argument

Engaged in parody but committed to the serious activity of philosophy, *Symposium* has been classified as an example of the "seriocomic"* genre: *spoudaiogeloion* in Greek.[1] As a seriocomic text, and noting its subsequent influence on Western intellectual culture as a whole, there can be no question that Plato executed his aims with great success. Blending poetry, rhetoric* and philosophy in a carefully constructed fictional setting, Plato challenges his audience to draw philosophical insight from an occasion which we might compare to a dinner party.

Symposium's playful literary qualities are one of its central aspects and the text became the model for all following works in the seriocomic genre.[2] Plato's aim was to educate while entertaining. In achieving this purpose, he fundamentally altered the discussion of the ways in which desire and erotic love were related to ethics, the pursuit of wisdom, and virtue.

Symposium has been adapted and referenced in so many different contexts over the last few millennia that its cultural legacy is extremely complex. What can safely be said, however, is that Plato is widely perceived as the intellectual father of the entire Western philosophical tradition.³ Even though *Symposium* is not a text that can be interpreted in a straightforward manner, its seven speeches on Eros* have provided continual inspiration for philosophers, theologians,* and scholars in other fields.

> "Symposium *has always been one of Plato's most read, most influential, and most imitated works. No doubt this has much to do with the universal appeal of its subject matter ... but it is also the rich variety of the work, together with its accessibility to readers with little philosophical training, which have given it a place of honour in the reception of Platonic ideas."*
> —— Richard Hunter, *Plato's Symposium*

Achievement in Context

It is difficult to reconstruct the original context in which *Symposium* would have been received. More than two thousand years have passed and there is little material evidence to help us. It is probably fair to assume, however, that the text's immediate audience would have been students of Plato's Academy,* the philosophical school he established in Athens. The fact that Plato founded the Academy indicates the richness of the intellectual culture of the Athens of the day. This must surely have contributed greatly to the work's success, providing an environment that was naturally receptive to Plato's philosophical discussions.

The value placed on philosophical discourse (the wider "conversation," so to speak) enabled Plato to flourish as a thinker and teacher. In *Symposium*, he contributed to this discourse by drawing on recent political, philosophical, and literary history in his vivid depiction of famous Athenian figures such as the philosopher Socrates,* the military general Alcibiades,* and the comic playwright Aristophanes.* This would have held significant appeal for his immediate audience.

Plato's students (notably Aristotle*) and others who wrote responses to the text such as Epicurus (a philosopher of the late fourth century b.c.e. and the founder of the Epicurean* school of philosophy) are responsible for securing its legacy. Epicurus believed the world was ruled by chance and that simple pleasures were to be highly valued. Both Epicurus and Aristotle wrote their own symposia in response to Plato's *Symposium*—although no specific details survive.[4]

Later in antiquity other philosophers such as Philo* and Plutarch* composed symposia modeled on Plato's. Both discussed some of the text's moral and ethical stances critically and used the style of the symposium for their own explorations of serious philosophical ideas in light-hearted settings.[5] Aristotle also responded (indirectly) to Plato's theory of Eros and virtue in his *Nicomachean Ethics*.[6]

Students of Plato's Academy, like Plutarch, continued to respond to the text long after Plato's death. Plutarch specifically focused on Plato's characterization of Eros as a daimon* (an intermediary spirit mediating between divine gods and mortal humans) to explore the role of the daimon in bridging the gap between divine and earthly spheres."[7]

In his work *On Isis and Osiris*,[8] Plutarch also drew on *Symposium* to defend a view of Greek and Egyptian cosmology—the science of the origin and development of the universe—that united Eros, in its divine form, with the Egyptian god Horus*—a religious fusion denoted by the term "syncretism."*

Limitations

Although Plato's *Symposium* explores ethical, philosophical, and cultural issues of the Athens of the early fourth century B.C.E., its literary and philosophical qualities have given it a universal appeal. Historically speaking, however, certain of its ideas have received more prominence than others. After all, different ages will have different priorities, biases and concerns.

With this in mind, it is worth noting the ways in which the text was received in the thinking of the Christian* era, especially after the attention given to it by Plotinus,* a philosopher of the third century C.E.,[9] and Augustine of Hippo,* a Christian thinker responsible for one of the most influential adaptations of *Symposium* for a Christian context. The Ascent to Beauty* in Socrates' speech is understood to be the foundation of Augustine of Hippo's theology* of love,[10] describing the progress of the Christian believer, as if on a ladder, ascending towards the love of the divine.

Centuries later, in the 1400s, the religious philosopher Marsilio Ficino* undertook a Christian retelling of *Symposium*, removing its emphasis on the erotic attraction of male bodies.[11] If this suppression of the more physical ideas about sexual desire and love was typical of the Christian mystical view of Plato's *Symposium*, such views have begun to be reclaimed by recent theorists of sexuality and gender.[12] In this we can say that core ideas from the text continue to organize many of the ways Western thought approaches questions concerning love, desire, and ethics.

---

1. Richard Hunter, *Plato's Symposium* (Oxford: Oxford University Press, 2004), 9.
2. Hunter, *Plato's Symposium,* 9–10, 126.
3. A. N. Whitehead, *Process and Reality: An Essay in Cosmology*, Corrected Edition (New York: The Free Press, 1978), 39.
4. Hunter, *Plato's Symposium*, 14–5.
5. Hunter, *Plato's Symposium*, 121–3; 125.
6. Aristotle, *The Nicomachean Ethics*, trans. David Ross (Oxford: Oxford University Press, 1980), 196–201; Richard Kraut, introduction to *The Blackwell Guide to Aristotle's Nicomachean Ethics*, ed. Richard Kraut (Oxford: Blackwell, 2006), 9; A. W. Price, *Love and Friendship in Plato and Aristotle* (Oxford: Oxford University Press, 1989), 85–6.
7. Robert Eisner, *The Road to Daulis: Psychoanalysis, Psychology and Classical Mythology* (Syracuse, NY: Syracuse University Press, 1987), 220, 222–3; Michele A. Luchesi, "Love Theory and Political Practice in Plutarch," in *Eros in Ancient Greece*, ed. Ed Sanders et al. (Oxford: Oxford University Press, 2013), 217–8.
8. Hunter, *Plato's Symposium,* 131–2.
9. Plotinus, "Love," in *The Enneads*, trans. Stephen MacKenna (London: Penguin Classics, 1991), 174–86; Hunter, *Plato's Symposium*, 130–1.
10. Bernard V. Brady, *Christian Love* (Washington D.C.: Georgetown University Press, 2003), 79.
11. Marsilio Ficino, *Commentary on Plato's 'Symposium' on Love*, trans. Sears Jayne (Dallas, TX: Spring Publications, 1985); Hunter, *Plato's Symposium*, 134.

12. See, for example, David Halperin, "Plato and the Erotics of Narrativity," in *Innovations of Antiquity,* ed. Daniel Selden and Ralph Hexter (New York, NY: Routledge, 1992), 95–126; Shannon Bell, "Tomb of the Sacred Prostitute: *Symposium,*" in *Shadow of Spirit: Postmodernism and Religion*, eds. Phillipa Berry and Andrew Wernick (London: Routledge, 1992), 198–210; Jeffrey Carnes, "The Myth Which is Not One: Construction of Discourse in Plato's Symposium," in *Rethinking Sexuality: Foucault and Classical Antiquity*, ed. David H. J. Larmour et al. (Princeton, NJ: Princeton University Press, 1998), 104–21.

MODULE 8
PLACE IN THE AUTHOR'S WORK

KEY POINTS
* Plato offers a comprehensive, if fragmented, philosophical vision across his works, addressing a wide range of topics.
* *Symposium,* usually dated to Plato's middle period, is linked thematically to his *Lysis* and *Phaedrus,* and to his wider ethical concerns.
* The text is one of Plato's most important and influential texts, particularly because of its distinctive literary form.

Positioning

Although the ordering of Plato's works is an imprecise science, *Symposium* is often held to be a product of his middle period, dating to around 380 b.c.e., when Plato was nearly 50 years of age.[1] In many of his earlier works that focused on questions of ethics and the living of a just life, he used the voice of his former teacher Socrates* to expose the assumptions and beliefs of those claiming to have knowledge.

In this period, Plato's thought seems to have extended to subjects such as the construction of an ideal political state (*The Republic*) and the nature of the soul (*Phaedo*). It is often thought that Plato's *Lysis* was composed before *Symposium*, which seems to refine and develop its central themes—love, desire, education and virtue—into a shorter text.[2]

In *Phaedrus*, Plato again investigates Eros,* beauty, and knowledge, adding to it a more detailed account of his Theory of Forms* and the idea that knowledge is a kind of recollection. Generally thought to have been composed after *Symposium*, *Phaedrus* offers a counterpoint to *Symposium*'s ideas. It appears to regard the madness of Eros, for example, as a force capable of provoking the recollection of the "ideal forms" experienced by the soul before birth and as something beneficial to attaining virtue. Socrates describes this madness as "the best of all forms of divine possession."[3]

For the Socrates who appears in Plato's *Phaedrus*, the desired body is more than a rung on a ladder, with loftier and more abstract ideas of love and beauty on the higher rungs.[4] Interpersonal human relationships are seen as valuable in their own right.[5] But it is worth noting that Plato's two central political texts, *The Republic* and the later *Laws*, come to different conclusions about the role of Eros in the stability of the state.[6]

> "[Symposium's] discussion of the nature and goals of loving relationships takes us to the heart of Plato's concern with the good life and how it is achieved."
> —— Frisbee C. C. Sheffield, "Introduction," Plato: The Symposium

Integration

Plato's body of work is one of the most significant achievements in the history of philosophy. Although it may be somewhat disparate and difficult to unify, being principally made up of dialogues that do not necessarily lend themselves to a single, authoritative interpretation, *Symposium* can only be properly understood as part of this corpus.

The task of interpreting Plato's work as a unified whole has occupied scholars for centuries. The modern debate on this subject is split between "developmentalist"* and "unitarian"* views.[7] According to the developmentalist stance, Plato's philosophy adopts different psychological, epistemological* and ethical positions as it evolves. According to the "unitarian" view, on the other hand, "there is a systematic unity of Platonic doctrine or belief among all the dialogues."[8]

The fact that these opposing views exist points to the difficulty of finding a clear and systematic set of doctrines in Plato's work. *Symposium*, as a work from his middle period, depicts ideas (among which are the Theory of Forms, the ways in which Eros is related to truth and justice, and the ways in which we might categorize and logically infer things) that are explored and debated in his other works. The most dramatically elaborate of all his dialogues,[9] *Symposium*'s unique significance in Plato's body of work lies in its pioneering literary form.

Significance

Plato is frequently regarded as the father of Western philosophy.[10] As one of his major dialogues, *Symposium*'s significance cannot really be questioned. It has proved to be a remarkably influential text from the time of its initial reception (and its frequent imitation) in antiquity* and throughout the Christian* era that followed. Having "shaped the way that the 'golden age' of classical Athens has been imagined,"[11] it continues to inform scholarship today.

It is perhaps ironic that what makes the text stand out from Plato's other writings (notably its highly literary form and its direct discussion of personal desire) are the very qualities that have sometimes undermined an appreciation of its philosophical richness:"Even those scholars who have read *Symposium* together with the *Phaedo* and the *Republic* as hallmarks of Platonism have had difficulties avoiding a highly selective approach to the text."[12]

Recent scholarship has, however, looked to show how the work's central concerns fit into Plato's thought as a whole. This has led to a renewed awareness of the ways in which the text's key elements are "intimately related to standard Platonic preoccupations: with the nature of the good life, with virtue and with how virtue is acquired and transmitted".[13]

---

1. K. Dover, "The Date of Plato's *Symposium*," *Phronesis* 10 (1965): 2–20.
2. Cf. Catherine Pickstock, "The Problem of Reported Speech: Friendship and Philosophy in Plato's *Lysis* and *Symposium*," *New Blackfriars* 82 (2001): 525–40.
3. Plato, *Phaedrus*, trans. Walter Hamilton (London: Penguin, 1973), 56.
4. Plato, *The Symposium*, 49–50.
5. Plato, *Phaedrus*, 64–5; A. W. Price, Love and Friendship in Plato and *Aristotle* (Oxford: Oxford University Press, 1989), 85–8.
6. Steven Berg, *Eros and the Intoxications of Enlightenment: On Plato's Symposium* (Albany, NY: State University of New York Press, 2010), 153.
7. William Prior, "Developmentalism," in *The Continuum Companion to Plato*, ed. Gerald A. Press (London: Continuum, 2012), 288–9.

8. Prior, "Developmentalism," 288.
9. Frisbee C. C. Sheffield, *Plato's Symposium: The Ethics of Desire* (Oxford: Oxford University Press, 2006), 3.
10. A. N. Whitehead, *Process and Reality: An Essay in Cosmology*, Corrected Edition (New York: The Free Press, 1978), 39.
11. Richard Hunter, *Plato's Symposium* (Oxford: Oxford University Press, 2004), 113.
12. Sheffield, *Plato's Symposium*, 3.
13. Sheffield, *Plato's Symposium*, 3.

SECTION 3
IMPACT

MODULE 9
THE FIRST RESPONSES

KEY POINTS

* The philosopher Xenophon* argues for a more functional conception of Eros* than Plato; Plato's student Aristotle* emphasizes the love of friendship over erotic love.
* Although it is not known how Plato responded to any critics in his lifetime, the account of Eros given in the later *Phaedrus* relates more to human relationships than that given in *Symposium*.
* The cultural context of Athens and the institutional context of Plato's Academy* allow us to assume that the text would have been the subject of vigorous debate during his lifetime.

Criticism

Our knowledge of critical responses to Plato's *Symposium* is limited both by our uncertainty about when it was written and by the fact that we have so few definite references to it from Plato's critics. Nevertheless, we can identify two strands of initial critical response.

The first of these is *Symposium*[1] of the philosopher Xenophon in which the "star" is, again, the philosopher Socrates.* Here, Xenophon has him sharing his wisdom on the subjects of Eros, virtue, and harmonious urban life.

Xenophon's Socrates presents himself as an expert matchmaker. His skill, we learn, is useful for uniting both people and cities. He is the sort of man who can "develop friendships between States and arrange suitable marriages, and would be a very suitable ally for both States and individuals to possess."[2] As in Plato's text, the philosophy is delivered with humor and irony—but Xenophon makes crucial modifications, and therefore implied criticisms, of Plato's ideas.

Although he acknowledges that the spiritual qualities and aspects of Eros transcend the physical, Xenophon chooses to emphasize the pragmatic value of its "lesser" form: *philia* (that is, the force of friendship, or the force of love associated with friendship). He does so by presenting a vision of love more personal, mutual and reciprocal* than that proposed by Plato's Socrates—and one supposedly more beneficial to the city, too.

The second strand of initial critical response to Plato's *Symposium* is that of his former student Aristotle whose *Nicomachean Ethics* is an indirect response to Plato's theory of Eros and virtue. Aristotle downplays the significance of Eros to the practice of philosophy and the virtuous life. For him, Eros is a force of instability, "a sort of excess of feeling,"[3] and while he argues that this can cement perfect friendship between two people, it is too intense to be shared among many. Instead, Aristotle emphasizes the less intense, more reciprocal love of *philia*: "the friendship of men who are good and alike in virtue."[4] Whereas Eros is associated with excess, *philia* is more like a "state of character."[5] In choosing *philia* as the glue that binds people and cities together in mutual virtue, Aristotle—like Xenophon—reacts against the more abstract and transcendental notion of Eros set out by Plato's Socrates in *Symposium*.[6]

> "One cannot be a friend to many people in the sense of having friendship of the perfect type with them, just as one cannot be in [erotic] love with many people at once (for [erotic] love is a sort of excess of feeling, and it is in the nature of such only to be felt towards one person)."
>
> —— Aristotle, *The Nicomachean Ethics*

Responses

The lack of documentary evidence of direct engagement between Plato and his audience makes it difficult to determine his responses to his critics.

Given that Plato's Academy was a place of learning, and that the intellectual culture of Athens was characterized by vigorous debate, we can assume a critical dialogue about Plato's *Symposium* and its treatment of Eros took place—even if we will never know the course it may have taken. However, it is possible to speculate on the nature of this debate by observing the ways in which Plato's treatment of Eros changes in his later work (although we must be careful not to definitively claim that these modifications were provoked by dialogue between the author and his critics).

Plato's *Phaedrus*, widely believed to have been composed after *Symposium*, is the best place to look. While this dialogue also investigates the role of Eros and *philia* in the pursuit of wisdom and virtue, Plato's presentation of Eros is altered from that of *Symposium*. It can still motivate and intellectually inspire the development of true understanding. But, unlike the vision of Socrates' speech in *Symposium*, the Eros of Plato's *Phaedrus* does not exist to usher the lover from the physical body of his beloved towards the sight of transcendental beauty. Now, both the lover and his beloved journey equally toward truth. As Plato explains, the beloved "experiences a counter-love which is the reflection of the love he inspires."[7]

Although this might seem to anticipate Aristotle's emphasis in his *Nicomachean Ethics* that perfect love be reciprocal—shared between two people[8]—Plato differs from Aristotle in his *Phaedrus*. For him, the "madness" of Eros leads to virtue by way of ethical inspiration. Aristotle, however, distrusts the "excess" of erotic love.[9]

Conflict and Consensus

The differences between Plato and Aristotle's ideas about the ideal form of love, and its role in the pursuit of wisdom and virtue, have occupied scholars throughout history. They continue to do so today.

Plato and Aristotle differ primarily on the significance each gives to erotic desire[10]—a topic of interest to different thinkers throughout history. The early Christian theologian St. Augustine,* for example, drew on Plato's description of the Ascent to Beauty,* making desire a central aspect of his theology* of love.[11] More recently, Pope Benedict XVI* drew on Symposium in his encyclical on love of 2005.[12] (An encyclical is a letter sent from the Pope to all bishops of the Roman Catholic Church.)* Benedict too emphasized the significance of erotic love, albeit in a Christianized form, in the pursuit of wisdom and truth.

Modern Plato scholarship has also sought to fully understand the emphasis on Eros in Symposium.[13] It is fair to say that an awareness of this aspect of the text has defined its critical reception and it is likely that it will continue to be its most debated feature.

---

1. Xenophon, *Conversations of Socrates*, trans. Hugh Tredennick and Robin Waterfield (London: Penguin, 1990).
2. Xenophon, *Conversations of Socrates,* 251.
3. Aristotle, *The Nicomachean Ethics*, trans. David Ross (Oxford: Oxford University Press, 1980), 201.
4. Aristotle, *The Nicomachean Ethics*, 196.
5. Aristotle, *The Nicomachean Ethics*, 200.
6. Richard Kraut, introduction to *The Blackwell Guide to Aristotle's Nicomachean Ethics*, 9.
7. Plato, *Phaedrus*, trans. Walter Hamilton (London: Penguin, 1973), 64.
8. A. W. Price, *Love and Friendship in Plato and Aristotle* (Oxford: Oxford University Press, 1989), 85–6; Catherine Pickstock, "The Problem of Reported Speech: Friendship and Philosophy in Plato's *Lysis* and *Symposium*," *New Blackfriars* 82 (2001): 525–40.
9. Plato, *Phaedrus*, 56; Aristotle, *The Nicomachean Ethics*, 201.
10. See, for example, Price, *Love and Friendship in Plato and Aristotle*.
11. Bernard V. Brady, *Christian Love* (Washington D.C.: Georgetown University Press, 2003), 79.
12. Benedict XVI, *Deus Caritas Est*, encyclical letter on Christian love, December 25, 2005, s.11.
13. See, for example, Frisbee C. C. Sheffield, *Plato's Symposium: The Ethics of Desire* (Oxford: Oxford University Press, 2006); Steven Berg, *Eros and the Intoxications of Enlightenment: On Plato's Symposium* (Albany, NY: State University of New York Press, 2010); Gary Alan Scott and William A. Welton, *Erotic Wisdom: Philosophy and Intermediacy in Plato's Symposium* (Albany, NY: State University of New York Press, 2008).

MODULE 10
THE EVOLVING DEBATE

KEY POINTS

- *Symposium* was the inspiration for a new type of philosophical writing.
- The dialogue's huge influence on Western thought and culture can be seen in Western philosophy, theology, literature, and poetry.
- The text recast discussions about love, desire, virtue, gender, and sexuality. It continues to shape these discussions today.

Uses and Problems

The distinctive literary form of Plato's *Symposium* proved to be particularly inspiring to later writers. The idea of the dinner party as a literary context for the discussion of philosophical ideas was striking enough to be imitated for a very long time. Indeed, Plato's work has been described as "the classic founding text of [a] genre."[1]

We can perhaps also thank *Symposium*, with its speeches given by spirited and humorously portrayed characters, for inspiring the tradition of the ancient novel. In the *Satyricon* of Petronius,* a Roman satirist of the first century c.e., we read tales of unrequited love told at a wild dinner party which recall Alcibiades'* speech in Plato's *Symposium*.[2] Similarly, *The Adventures of Leucippe and Clitophon* by Achilles Tatius* and the *Metamorphoses* of Apuleius* (both writers of the second century c.e.) adapt Plato's innovations for a different audience, notably replacing the homosexual model of desire and virtue with its heterosexual equivalent.³

The central question of the text—the place of erotic desire in the search for wisdom and virtue—continued to be important to later Greek schools of philosophy categorized together as "Hellenistic."* Zeno* and other early Stoic* thinkers emphasized that Eros could be beneficial to ethics. These thinkers were part of a school of philosophy, Stoicism, that believed the virtuous life is best lived in accordance with nature, indifferent to pain and pleasure. The Stoics sought "to improve on Plato's own conception of Eros in *Symposium* by further uniting it with education."⁴ Christian* thinkers would later develop these themes.

The origin of Christian interpretations of Plato's *Symposium* may be traced back to Plotinus,* a "Neoplatonist" philosopher of the third century c.e. Neoplatonism was a mystical, philosophical, and religious system deeply influenced by Plato's works. Plotinus laid the ground for the subsequent Christian tradition of viewing the Ascent to Beauty* as a pagan counterpart to the ascent of the Christian soul to heaven.⁵

Plato's ideas about Eros were adapted for a Christian context by early theologians* such as Origen of Alexandria,* Gregory of Nyssa,* and Augustine of Hippo,* in the third to fifth centuries c.e. Augustine's account of love, for example, is strongly influenced by the passages concerning the Ascent to Beauty, with this image forming a basis for his theology of love.⁶ In the European period known as the Renaissance (roughly the fourteenth to the sixteenth centuries), *Symposium* was translated by the Italian Leonardo Bruni.* His version, which censored the more bawdy and physical depictions of Eros, had great influence on the seminal (but rather sanitized) Christian retelling of the text by the Catholic scholar Marsilio Ficino.*7

> "Symposium *became the foundational text for all literary dinner parties which followed."*
>
> —— Richard Hunter, *Plato's Symposium*

Schools of Thought

Plato's ideas have had a formative influence on all Western thought and culture, especially as a result of their passage into Christian theology through the work of figures such as Augustine of Hippo. They began to re-enter wide circulation in their own right from the Renaissance onwards as artists and intellectuals alike took notice of them. Poets of the nineteenth century, such as Percy Bysshe Shelley,* used Plato's discussions of Eros to define Romantic love.[8] Important writers of the twentieth century have similarly engaged directly with Plato's *Symposium*. In his novel *Maurice*, E. M. Forster* used *Symposium* to explore questions of homosexuality, treating Plato as a lens through which to look at the spiritual and the physical conceptions of Eros, as demonstrated by the contrasting characters of Socrates and Alcibiades* respectively.[9]

Philosophers of all kinds have continued to return to Plato into the twentieth and twenty-first centuries. Among them are Continental Philosopher* such as Martin Heidegger,* Jacques Derrida,* and Michel Foucault.*[10] Modern Platonists in the analytic* tradition adopt a logical and scientific approach to philosophical problems. They take their epistemological* orientation (focusing on the nature and scope of knowledge and how it is acquired) from Plato's theory of the Forms of Beauty,* Truth and Goodness. This theory sees these attributes as transcendental features that exist beyond those objects of the world that we can perceive with our sense organs—"sensible" objects.

According to this view (held to various degrees by philosophers such as Gottlob Frege,* Bertrand Russell,* Hilary Putnam,* and most recently Saul Kripke*), sensible objects function as versions of these abstract forms.[11]

Ideas from *Symposium* have also been adapted by theorists of psychoanalysis,* such as Sigmund Freud* and Jacques Lacan,* to express concepts of desire.[12] Film, art, and opera, too, have frequently turned to *Symposium*, whether in the painting of Peter Paul Rubens* that depicts the moment of Alcibiades'* dramatic arrival at Plato's dinner party,[13] or the film *Hedwig and the Angry Inch** (2001), which engages with Aristophanes'* myth of human desire and the longing to be rejoined to one's other half.

In Current Scholarship

In the present day, Plato's *Symposium* continues to have a wide influence on scholarship. Classical philosophers, scholars of Plato,[14] and Christian* theologians continue, unsurprisingly, to discuss and analyze the work.[15] Literary theorists such as Roland Barthes* have also found much to interest them in Plato's text, particularly in the dialogue's open-ended construction and the complex and ambiguous interactions between the speeches.[16]

Contemporary theorists of gender and sexuality, such as David Halperin,* have noted the work's unusual presentation of sex in the speech of Aristophanes.[17] This has led to debate over the extent to which Plato's ancient text can be taken as a model for contemporary norms of gender and sexual preference. Halperin himself has been keen to stress how modern understandings of sexual orientation do not match the more fluid sense of sexuality that characterized ancient Greece. There is little evidence of a distinct gay culture in ancient Greece, for example, and elite males such as those depicted in Plato's *Symposium* found that having sexual relationships with men was not incompatible with being married to a woman for the purpose of having children.[18]

Halperin has also argued that Aristophanes' speech "stops short of deriving a distinction between homo-and heterosexuality from his own myth just when the logic of his analysis would seem to have driven him ineluctably to it. The omission is telling."[19] This is an important and on-going debate.

---

1. Richard Hunter, *Plato's Symposium* (Oxford: Oxford University Press, 2004), 15.
2. Hunter, *Plato's Symposium*, 126.
3. Hunter, *Plato's Symposium*, 122–3, 127–9.
4. Bernard Collette-Ducic, "Making Friends: The Stoic Conception of Love and Its Platonic Background," in *Ancient and Medieval Concepts of Friendship*, eds. Suzanne Stern-Gillet and Gary M. Gurtler SJ (Albany, NY: State University of New York Press, 2014), 108.
5. Plotinus, "Love," in *The Enneads*, trans. Stephen MacKenna (London: Penguin Classics, 1991), 174–86; Hunter, *Plato's Symposium*, 130–1.
6. Bernard V. Brady, *Christian Love* (Washington D.C.: Georgetown University Press, 2003), 79.
7. Marsilio Ficino, *Commentary on Plato's 'Symposium' on Love*, trans. Sears Jayne (Dallas, TX:

Spring Publications, 1985); Hunter, *Plato's Symposium*, 134.

8. Hunter, *Plato's Symposium*, 123–4.
9. E. M. Forster, *Maurice* (London: Penguin, 2005). Hunter, *Plato's Symposium*, 115–7.
10. For a summary, see Drew Hyland, *Questioning Platonism: Continental Interpetations of Plato* (Albany, NY: State University of New York Press, 2004).
11. See Mark Balaguer, "Platonism in Metaphysics," in *The Stanford Encyclopedia of Philosophy*, Spring 2014 Edition, ed. Edward N. Zalta, accessed April 1, 2015, <http://plato.stanford.edu/archives/spr2014/ entries/platonism/>.
12. Sigmund Freud, *Beyond the Pleasure Principle*, trans. James Strachey (London and New York: W. W. Norton, 1961), 52; Jacques Lacan, *Écrits: The First Complete Edition in English*, trans. Bruce Fink (New York & London: W. W. Norton, 2006), 699–700; Hunter, *Plato's Symposium*, 117–9.
13. Elizabeth McGrath, "'The Drunken Acibiades': Rubens's Picture of Plato's Symposium," *Journal of the Warburg and Courtauld Institutes* 46 (1983): 228–35.
14. See, for example, Hunter, *Plato's Symposium*; Frisbee C. C. Sheffield, *Plato's Symposium: The Ethics of Desire* (Oxford: Oxford University Press, 2006); Steven Berg, *Eros and the Intoxications of Enlightenment: On Plato's Symposium* (Albany, NY: State University of New York Press, 2010).
15. For example: Catherine Pickstock, "The Problem of Reported Speech: Friendship and Philosophy in Plato's *Lysis* and *Symposium*," *New Blackfriars* 82 (2001): 525–40; Benedict XVI, *Deus Caritas Est*, encyclical letter on Christian love, December 25, 2005, s.11.
16. Hunter, *Plato's Symposium*, 113; Roland Barthes, *A Lover's Discourse: Fragments*, trans. Richard Howard (London: Vintage, 2002). See also, Jeffrey Carnes, "The Myth Which is Not One: Construction of Discourse in Plato's Symposium," in *Rethinking Sexuality: Foucault and Classical Antiquity*, ed. David H. J. Larmour et al. (Princeton, NJ: Princeton University Press, 1998), 104–21.
17. See, for example, David Halperin, "Plato and the Erotics of Narrativity," in *Innovations of Antiquity*, ed. Daniel Selden and Ralph Hexter (New York, NY: Routledge, 1992), 95–126.
18. David Halperin, *One Hundred Years of Homosexuality: and Other Essays on Greek Love* (London: Routledge, 1990), 15–40.
19. Halperin, *One Hundred Years of Homosexuality*, 18–9.

MODULE 11
IMPACT AND INFLUENCE TODAY

KEY POINTS

- *Symposium* is one of the classic texts of Western philosophy.
- Plato's emphasis on erotic desire in his account of love continues to challenge contemporary thinkers.
- Critics argue that Plato's account of love is insufficiently reciprocal* and leaves too little room for simple affection.

Position

Symposium, a text largely responsible for Plato's reputation as one of the fathers of Western philosophy, is a work of great philosophical and literary originality.[1] Given the extent of its influence on Western thought and culture over more than two thousand years, we should not be surprised that scholars continue to turn to it. The history of how the text has been received and what it reveals about the author and the age in which he lived are interesting in different ways.

What is perhaps surprising is the extent to which the work continues to be used creatively by modern scholars working in a variety of disciplines. Psychoanalysts,*[2] poststructuralist* literary critics,[3] and theorists of gender and sexuality[4] have all turned to it in recent decades, sometimes engaging with the more "traditional" fields of philosophy and theology in their research. Research like this, drawing on methods and theories from across disciplines, is known as "interdisciplinary" in approach. As an example of where interdisciplinary engagement might lead, a Christian* theologian has recently drawn on literary analysis to explore the ways in which the complex construction of *Symposium* is intended as a reminder of the "precariousness and partiality of our attainment to truth."[5]

The fact that the text is still relevant today was recently confirmed when it was used in a court case in the American state of Colorado. Academics were called to debate the view of homosexuality offered by *Symposium* as part of a case about constitutional* amendments and the rights of homosexuals in the present day.[6]

> "The safest general characterization of the European philosophical tradition is that it consists of a series of footnotes to Plato."
>
> —— A. N. Whitehead, *Process and Reality: An Essay on Cosmology*

Interaction

Symposium continues to provoke debate among philosophers and theologians on whether its account of erotic love leaves room for affection between people (an argument made recently by the classical scholar GregoryVlastos,* for example)[7] or whether the form of love it endorses is somewhat impersonal.

The roots of the debate are genuinely ancient—Plato and Aristotle differed in their ideas about what constitutes ideal love, with Aristotle favoring *philia* (the more reciprocal love of friendship) and Plato favoring Eros.* But Plato's emphasis on erotic desire in his analysis of love has continued to challenge contemporary thought. The Danish theologian Anders Nygren,* for example, dismisses Platonic love (and indeed the Eros of the ancient Greeks in general) as fundamentally acquisitive—that is,"self-seeking."[8]

Scholars such as Catherine Osborne have defended Plato from the criticisms of the likes of Vlastos and Nygren by arguing that Plato's account of Eros does in fact provide a basis for a richly interpersonal form of love.[9] Catherine Pickstock has argued that an appreciation of this aspect of the work requires an attentiveness to the "unusual 'literary' devices"[10] that Plato uses, which have often been overlooked by critics. She suggests that the critics have employed a reading of the text that is too literal and fails to appreciate the significance of its disjointed, narrative form for its meaning. Prioritizing how the text itself is structured allows us to see that, for Plato, "friendship itself is structured as a set of friendly exchanges."[11]

The Continuing Debate

Critics of Plato's account of erotic love have engaged with his texts directly, and also opposed the traditions of thought that he has influenced. In the first case, engaging directly with *Symposium*, Gregory Vlastos has argued that Plato presents love of persons simply as a means of reaching something higher, specifically the contemplation of the Beautiful in itself (Vlastos derives this from the Ascent to Beauty* section of Socrates'* speech). So people are regarded merely as instruments, as "placeholders of the predicates 'useful' and 'beautiful'," and Plato "relegate[s] love of persons to the lowest level" in his hierarchy.[12] Vlastos then looks at Aristotle's account of ideal love, which, he says, teaches that "to love another person is to wish for that person's good for that person's sake."[13] Vlastos sees Aristotle's account as far superior to that of Plato.

In turn, Anders Nygren has focused his critique on the ancient Greek concept of Eros in general, and on those forms of Christian theology that, building on Plato, have sought to find a central place for Eros in their theologies of love. Nygren regards erotic desire as basically "egocentric," or self-seeking, and sees this as a deeply inadequate form of love.[14] By contrast, in his view true love is one that purifies itself of any self-seeking motivation. He therefore opposes forms of Christian theology that emphasize Eros, and defends an alternative theology that presents self-sacrificial love as the only "truly" Christian love.[15]

---

1. Richard Hunter, *Plato's Symposium* (Oxford: Oxford University Press, 2004), 113.
2. Hunter, *Plato's Symposium*, 117–9.
3. Shannon Bell, "Tomb of the Sacred Prostitute: *Symposium,*" in *Shadow of Spirit: Postmodernism and Religion*, eds. Phillipa Berry and Andrew Wernick (London: Routledge, 1992), 198–210; Paul Allen Miller, "The Classical Roots of Poststructuralism: Lacan, Derrida, and Foucault," *International Journal of the Classical Tradition* 5 (1998): 209–13.
4. David Halperin, "Plato and the Erotics of Narrativity," in *Innovations of Antiquity*, ed. Daniel Selden and Ralph Hexter (New York, NY: Routledge, 1992), 95–126; Jeffrey Carnes, "The Myth Which is Not One: Construction of Discourse in Plato's Symposium," in *Rethinking Sexuality: Foucault and Classical Antiquity*, ed. David H. J. Larmour et al. (Princeton, NJ: Princeton University Press, 1998), 104–21.
5. Catherine Pickstock, "The Problem of Reported Speech: Friendship and Philosophy in Plato's *Lysis* and *Symposium,*" *New Blackfriars* 82 (2001): 535.
6. Hunter, *Plato's Symposium,* 125; Martha Nussbaum, "Platonic Love and Colorado Law: the

Relevance of Ancient Greek Norms to Modern Sexual Controversies," *Virginia Law Review* 80 (1994): 1515–651.
7. Gregory Vlastos, "The Individual as an Object of Love in Plato," in *Platonic Studies,* ed. Gregory Vlastos (Princeton NJ: Princeton University Press, 1973), 3–42.
8. Anders Nygren, *Agape and Eros*, trans. Philip Watson (London: SPCK, 1983).
9. Catherine Osborne, *Eros Unveiled: Plato and the God of Love* (Oxford: Clarendon Press, 1994), 222–6; see also Pickstock, "The Problem of Reported Speech," 525–40.
10. Pickstock, "The Problem of Reported Speech," 526.
11. Pickstock, "The Problem of Reported Speech," 530.
12. Vlastos, "The Individual as an Object of Love in Plato," 26.
13. Vlastos, "The Individual as an Object of Love in Plato," 3.
14. Nygren, *Agape and Eros*, 210.
15. Nygren, *Agape and Eros*, 559–60, 721.

MODULE 12
WHERE NEXT?

KEY POINTS

- As a foundational text of Western philosophy, *Symposium*'s importance is unlikely to decline.
- The text's emphasis on erotic desire, its complex narrative structure, and its innovative ideas about gender and sexuality continue to excite scholars.
- The text's striking philosophical insights, its original literary qualities, and the manner of its reception in Western civilization mean we must consider it a seminal work.

Potential

Plato's *Symposium* is a seminal text in Western literature and will almost certainly continue to be relevant. Almost 2,500 years after it was written, people still turn to the work to better understand both ancient Greece and its cultural concerns and the manner in which Plato's ideas have shaped theories of love, desire, and ethics. When we study the different ways in which *Symposium* has been used over many centuries to explain the love of God as the model for love between people, for example, we learn as much about European cultural history as we learn about the text itself.

Scholars of Plato, philosophers, and theologians* continue to consult the text to solve the questions it poses about erotic desire and what the ideal of love might be. But *Symposium*'s influence permeates Western culture beyond questions of scholarship. We can see it in cultural assumptions about love and desire, and the relationship of these things to wisdom, virtue, and happiness. We have seen how *Symposium* has shaped poetry and literature, visual art, and film.

Over the last century, furthermore, there have been innovative uses of the text by psychoanalysts* such as Sigmund Freud* and Jacques Lacan,* by poststructuralist* literary theorists such Roland Barthes,* and by theorists of gender and sexuality such as Michel Foucault* and David Halperin.*

The use of elaborate literary devices to express profound philosophical arguments makes *Symposium* a complex and enigmatic text that continues to inspire in many contexts. A representative symbol of the unique genius of Plato's literary and philosophical project, *Symposium* will be considered an important work for as long as Western civilization continues to turn to its past to understand itself.

> "Plato's Symposium *holds unique interest for modern readers. Arguably, no other Platonic dialogue combines a topic of so central importance to Plato's thought with so dramatic a depiction of renowned ancient characters."*
>
> —— Gary Alan Scott and William A. Welton, *Erotic Wisdom: Philosophy and Intermediacy in Plato's Symposium*

Future Directions

A new generation of Plato scholars is re-exploring the meaning of Plato's emphasis on the erotic and shedding new light on its significance for ancient Greece and the world of today.[1] Some have seen the text's unusual literary characteristics as the key to its interpretation.² In addition, some of the most creative responses to the text have come from theorists of literature, gender, and sexuality. The French cultural theorist Michel Foucault's celebrated three-volume *History of Sexuality*, for example, published in the early 1980s, prompted a number of scholars to return to the subject of antiquity,* and in particular to Plato's *Symposium*, which Foucault discusses in volume two.³ Their aim was to clarify, dispute, and engage with Foucault's theoretical framework and findings.

The theories of desire proposed in the speech that Plato gives to the playwright Aristophanes,* (the myth that human beings have been split in half and are now driven by desire for reunion) have become a focal point in this debate.⁴ Plato's imagining of our sexual orientation as dependent on the composition of our prior whole (either male-female, male-male, or female-female) has been of interest to modern theorists of sexuality such as David Halperin, the American author of *One Hundred Years of Homosexuality*, a collection of essays discussing Greek sexuality.⁵

Aristophanes' myth of split souls is relevant to more recent arguments relating to sexual and gender identity and the extent to which our sexuality is formed by culture and questions of biological determinism* and social construction.* Biological determinism is the theory that individual human characteristics are genetically determined. Social construction is the theory that human values and preferences, including sexual orientation, are determined by the social and cultural context we live in. It has been argued that *Symposium* is far more radical than people might have realized. Perhaps it recasts "sex into a form of philosophy" so that "with Plato and for Plato, we remake sex."[6]

Likewise, feminist thinkers have looked to Plato's *Symposium* to find a stronger acknowledgement of female sexuality. It has been suggested that Plato offers glimpses of a more inclusive vision of femininity and the possibilities of feminine knowledge according to which women are not defined by a disempowering "lack" decided by culture on their behalf.[7] According to this view, Plato paves the way toward a theory of sexuality that might help us resist the models of sex and gender that arose after him.

Summary

Plato's *Symposium* gave rise to a new type of philosophical literature: the seriocomic* dinner party where weighty philosophical ideas are discussed in a lighthearted manner. It has attracted many imitators, both ancient and modern.[8] Within its dynamic and lively portrait of memorable historical figures such as Socrates,* Aristophanes, and Alcibiades,* there exist passages of philosophical speculation, myths of human sexuality, and examinations of the relationship between the passion of Eros* and ethics. These subjects have fascinated readers and critics for thousands of years.

Symposium is a text that contains some of Plato's finest literary writing, combining metaphor and parody, lucid reasoning, and rhetorical* showmanship. Philosophical ideas that occur elsewhere in Plato's work, such as the theory of Intelligible Forms* that exist outside of the world we can perceive with our senses, are deployed here with a remarkable lyricism. The speech that Plato gives to

Socrates on the spiritual journey from bodily erotic desire to the sight of the abstract Form of Beauty* has had an enormous influence on much of Western thought and culture, notably Christian.

The significance of *Symposium* extends beyond Plato's ideas and the form in which he chose to express them. The work's reception over time and the depth of its cultural influence onWestern civilization as a whole mean it continues to be one of the greatest-ever works in the arts and humanities.

---

1. See, for example, Frisbee C. C. Sheffield, *Plato's Symposium: The Ethics of Desire* (Oxford: Oxford University Press, 2006); Steven Berg, *Eros and the Intoxications of Enlightenment: On Plato's Symposium* (Albany, NY: State University of New York Press, 2010); Gary Alan Scott and William A. Welton, *Erotic Wisdom: Philosophy and Intermediacy in Plato's Symposium* (Albany, NY: State University of New York Press, 2008).
2. See, for example, Catherine Pickstock, "The Problem of Reported Speech: Friendship and Philosophy in Plato's *Lysis* and *Symposium*," *New Blackfriars* 82 (2001): 125–40.
3. Michel Foucault, *The Use of Pleasure*, vol. 2 of *The History of Sexuality,* trans. Robert Hurley (New York: Random House, 1990), 230–3, 235–42.
4. Plato, *The Symposium*, in Plato: The Symposium, trans. M. C. Howatson, ed. M. C. Howatson and Frisbee C. C. Sheffield (Cambridge: Cambridge University Press, 2008), 22–7.
5. David Halperin, *One Hundred Years of Homosexuality: and Other Essays on Greek Love* (London: Routledge, 1990), 15–40; Jeffrey Carnes, "The Myth Which is Not One: Construction of Discourse in Plato's Symposium," in *Rethinking Sexuality: Foucault and Classical Antiquity*, ed. David H. J. Larmour et al. (Princeton, NJ: Princeton University Press, 1998), 104–21.
6. Carnes, "The Myth Which is Not One", 120.
7. Shannon Bell, "Tomb of the Sacred Prostitute: *Symposium*," in *Shadow of Spirit: Postmodernism and Religion*, eds. Phillipa Berry and Andrew Wernick (London: Routledge, 1992), 198–210; Anne-Marie Bowery, "Diotima Tells Socrates a Story: A Narrative Analysis of Plato's *Symposium*," in *Feminism and Ancient Philosophy*, ed. Julie K. Ward (London: Routledge, 1996), 175–94.
8. Richard Hunter, *Plato's Symposium* (Oxford: Oxford University Press, 2004), 9–10.

GLOSSARY OF TERMS

1. **Academy:** an influential philosophical school founded by Plato in about 387 B.C.E. in a place just outside Athens, sacred because it was the burial ground of the ancient hero Academus. It flourished until about 87 B.C.E.

2. **Analytic philosophy:** a branch of contemporary philosophy considered dominant in Anglo-American philosophical research, and often contrasted in style and method with "Continental philosophy." It adopts a logical and scientific approach to philosophical problems, insisting on the need for the verification of information through the use of rigorous proofs borrowed from mathematics and logic.

3. **Antiquity:** the period of ancient history, particularly referring in common usage to the "classical" civilizations prior to the Middle Ages, especially those of Greece and Rome.

4. **Ascent to Beauty:** according to Plato, Eros can give us the desire to climb, as if on a ladder, from the sight of a beautiful body to the sight of the eternal Form of Beauty itself. The first "rung" of the ladder in the Ascent to Beauty is the love of a beautiful body. The intermediate stages are an appreciation of all beautiful bodies, the love of beautiful souls, the love of the beauty of institutions and laws, and the love of the beauty of knowledge; the final rung is the sight of the Form of Beauty itself and the true virtue this sight affords.

5. **Biological determinism:** the theory that individual human characteristics, including sexual and other preferences, are genetically determined.

6. **Christian:** relating to Christianity, a global religion based on the teachings of Jesus Christ and the Bible. It is one of the three great "monotheistic" (belief in one God) religious systems, along with Judaism and Islam.

7. **Civic identity:** those things that define the position and obligations of a person who lives in an urban place (in this case, the city-state of ancient Athens).

8. **Constitutional:** concerning a set of established principles for the governing of a nation or state (such as the US constitution).

9. **Continental philosophy:** the branch of contemporary philosophy dominant in Continental Europe throughout the twentieth century, and usually distinguished

in style and methodology from the "analytic philosophy" dominant in Anglo-American philosophy.

10. **Daimon:** in ancient Greek thought and belief, a daimon was an intermediary supernatural being who often communicated between the gods and humanity.

11. **Developmentalist:** the scholarly view that Plato's philosophy developed throughout his work as he modified his philosophical and psychological positions.

12. **Disputation:** the skill and techniques required to win a public debate through persuasion.

13. **Eleusinian Mysteries:** secret religious rites that took place at Eleusis in ancient Greece for initiation into the cult of the goddesses Demeter and Persephone.

14. **Epic poems:** long poems, which typically in ancient literature, narrated in poetic form a story or legend related to some heroic figure.

15. **Epicureanism:** an ancient school of philosophy founded in Athens by the philosopher Epicurus that viewed the world as ruled by chance and saw simple forms of pleasure as the highest good.

16. **Epistemology:** the subdiscipline of philosophy concerned with the nature and scope of knowledge, and the methods by which knowledge may be acquired.

17. **Equivocal:** open to interpretation; ambiguous. Eros was considered an "equivocal" force since it was difficult to say for certain whether its effects were positive or negative.

18. **Eros:** the ancient Greek word for the form of love associated with sexual desire, from which the modern term "erotic" is derived.

19. **Ethnography:** the scientific description of peoples and cultures, with their customs, habits, and points of difference.

20. **Form of Beauty:** the unchanging and eternal "essence" of beauty, described by Plato as a "wondrous vision"; the sight of the Form of Beauty affords true virtue.

21. **Hedonism:** the doctrine or theory of ethics in which pleasure is regarded as the chief good, or the proper end of action.

22. **Hedwig and the Angry Inch:** an award-winning American film of 2001 directed and adapted from his own stage play by John Cameron Mitchell. The film makes frequent references to Aristophanes' speech in *The Symposium*.
23. **Hellenistic philosophy:** the various schools of thought that arose in Hellenistic (ancient Greek) civilization after Aristotle, including Stoicism, Epicureanism, and ending with Neo-Platonism.
24. **Horus:** a god who, in ancient Egyptian mythology, protected the monarchy, frequently depicted as a man with the head of a falcon.
25. **Intelligible Forms:** ideas that can be perceived by the intellect and which structure human understanding.
26. **Metaphysics:** a subdiscipline of philosophy studying the fundamental structures of reality.
27. **Mystical:** concerning religious mysticism, that is, spiritual forms of religious belief, practice or experience that are said to exceed ordinary human understanding.

28. **Neoplatonism:** a religious and philosophical school of the third century C.E. derived from a mixture of the philosophy of Plato and various mystical traditions.
29. **Peloponnesian War:** a war between the city-states of Sparta and Athens and their respective empires between 431 B.C.E. and 404 B.C.E., ending in victory for the Spartans.
30. **Polyphony:** a term used to describe the effect of the "many voices" that speak in *The Symposium*.
31. **Polytheism:** worshipping or believing in more than one god.
32. **Poststructuralism:** a body of philosophical and critical work of the twentieth century. Poststructuralists disagree with the theoretical position held by "structuralism" that a text's meaning is found in definite narrative, interpretative, and linguistic structures.
33. **Psychoanalysis:** a theory of mind, developed by Sigmund Freud, defined by a method of treatment that attempts to access and interpret the unconscious.

34. **Pythagoreanism:** a system of philosophical and religious thought and practice deriving from the teachings of the Greek philosopher and mathematician Pythagoras (570–c.495 B.C.E.), based on the idea that reality is fundamentally mathematical in nature.
35. **Reciprocal:** done in return, or concerning exchange.
36. **Rhetoric:** the art of discourse, or of persuasive speaking and writing. As a discipline for instructing students in the effective use of language, it has held a central place in the European intellectual tradition from the classical world to the present day.
37. **Roman Catholic Church:** the largest Christian Church and one of the oldest religious institutions in the world, led by the Pope.
38. **Seriocomic:** concerning a type of literature that combines both serious and comic elements.
39. **Silenus:** a minor rural god in ancient Greek religion associated with the major god Dionysus and the activities of dancing and making wine.
40. **Social construction:** the theory that human values and preferences, including sexual orientation, are determined by the social and cultural context in which someone lives.
41. **Sophists:** paid teachers of philosophy and rhetoric in ancient Greece; often associated with moral relativism, skepticism, and superficial and disingenuous forms of reasoning.
42. **Sparta:** a Greek city-state in in the fifth century B.C.E. It defeated Athens in the Peloponnesian War to become the most important city in Greece.
43. **Stoicism:** an ancient Greek school of philosophy founded in Athens by Zeno of Citium, which taught that the virtuous life is lived in accordance with nature, and is indifferent to the transience of pain, pleasure and fortune.
44. **Syncretism:** the joining together or attempted joining together of different systems of belief into a new whole.
45. **Theologian:** a scholar engaged in the study of the nature and works of God.

46. **Theory of Forms:** according to Plato's Theory of Forms, everything we are able to perceive with our sense organs is an image or impression of its non-material "Form"—its unchanging, essential counterpart in the "world of Forms." Plato understands the Forms to be the highest and most fundamental kind of reality, but practically impossible to grasp without the most highly refined knowledge.
47. **Treatise:** a written text systematically investigating a particular subject (such as a treatise on theology or philosophy).
48. **Unitarian:** the scholarly view that Plato's philosophical doctrine and belief are consistent across all his works.

PEOPLE MENTIONED IN THE TEXT

1. **Achilles Tatius** was a Greek writer of the second century c.e. Little is known about him apart from his novel *Leucippe and Clitophon*, which imitated stylistic aspects of Plato's *Symposium*.

2. **Agathon (448–400 b.c.e.)** was a renowned Greek playwright of tragedies, and a character in Plato's *Symposium*. Although none of his plays survives, we know that in 416 b.c.e., when *Symposium* is set, Agathon would have been celebrating his success at the Lenaia festival in Athens.

3. **Alcaeus of Mytilene** was a Greek lyric poet of the sixth century b.c.e. from the island of Lesbos. Although his poetry covers a variety of subjects, he is most noted for the surviving fragments that concern politics and hymns to the gods.

4. **Al-Farabi (870–950 c.e)** was an Islamic philosopher from Turkestan who studied in Baghdad and travelled widely around the Islamic world. His major philosophical treatise *al-Madina al fadila (The Virtuous City)* is a thorough and detailed engagement with many ideas in Plato's *Republic*. His work exerted considerable influence upon later Islamic philosophers.

5. **Alcibiades (450–404 b.c.e.)** was a notorious Athenian general, orator and politician, and a character in Plato's *Symposium*. Known as a brilliant military strategist with a flamboyant personality, he was forced to flee Athens not long after the setting of *Symposium,* and advised her great enemies Sparta and Persia before being assassinated.

6. **Apuleius (125–80 c.e.)** was a Latin-language writer and orator who had studied Platonic philosophy. He is known for his risqué satirical novel the *Metamorphosis*, also known as *The Golden Ass*.

7. **Aristophanes (circa 446–386 b.c.e.)** was an Athenian comic playwright who features in Plato's *Symposium*. Of his 40 known plays, 11 survive, including *The Clouds*, a play about philosophy and sophistry that portrayed Socrates in a negative light.

8. **Aristotle (384–322 b.c.e.)** was an ancient Greek philosopher and student of Plato. He wrote many treatises, the most famous of which are his *Nicomachean Ethics* and his *Metaphysics*. His philosophical work builds, adapts, and expands

on the legacy of Plato.

9. **Augustine of Hippo (354–430 c.e.)**, also known as St. Augustine, was a highly influential early Christian theologian, philosopher, and bishop of the Church. His theology, represented in key works such as *Confessions* and *The City of God*, drew on and adapted Platonic and Neoplatonic ideas.

10. **Roland Barthes (1915–80)** was an important French literary theorist and philosopher, who explored ideas around structuralism, poststructuralism and semiotics (the analysis of signs). His works include *Mythologies* and *A Lover's Discourse*, the latter of which draws heavily on Plato's *Symposium*.

11. **Benedict XVI (b. 1927, as Joseph Ratzinger)** is a German Roman Catholic theologian and priest. He was Pope of the Roman Catholic Church from 2005 until 2013.

12. **Leonardo Bruni (1369–1444)** was an Italian humanist and historian who worked in Florence. He was a notable historian of both antiquity and his own period, and produced a new translation of Plato's *Symposium*.

13. **Jacques Derrida (1930–2004)** was a highly influential French Continental philosopher who developed a form of semiotic analysis (the analysis of signs) known as "deconstruction." His most famous works include *Of Grammatology* and *Writing and Difference*.

14. **Empedocles (490–430 b.c.e.)** was a philosopher from Acragas in Sicily. Sections from two of his major works—the *Purifications* and *On Nature*—survive.

15. **Eryximachus (circa. 448–late fifth or early fourth century b.c.e.)** was an Athenian doctor who features as a character in Plato's *Symposium*.

16. **Euripides (480–406 b.c.e.)** was an ancient Greek playwright. He is reputed to have written over 90 plays, mainly tragedies, and was one of the most important figures in the cultural world of classical Athens.

17. **Marsilio Ficino (1433–99)** was a key figure in the early Italian Renaissance. He both translated all the known works of Plato into Latin and wrote commentaries on them. He famously retold *Symposium* in his *De Amore*, "On Love," in a way

that sought to combine Platonic and Christian ideas.

18. **E. M. Forster (1879–1970)** was an English novelist. He is known primarily for his novels *A Room with a View, Howards End* and *A Passage to India*.

19. **Michel Foucault (1926–84)** was a French philosophical and cultural historian. His work, focusing on theories of power and knowledge, included a notable study of the history of sexuality in which he engaged with Plato's *Symposium*.

20. **Gottlob Frege (1848–1925)** was a German philosopher renowned for his contribution to analytic philosophy in the fields of logic and language. He is famous for works such as *The Foundations of Arithmetic*.

21. **Sigmund Freud (1856–1939)** was an Austrian neurologist who is acknowledged as the father of psychoanalysis. Of his many books, among the most famous are *Totem and Taboo, Beyond the Pleasure Principle* and *Civilization and its Discontents*.

22. **Gregory of Nyssa (335–94 c.e.)** was an influential theologian and bishop of the early Christian Church from Cappadocia. He incorporated Platonic and Neo-Platonic ideas into his theology in works such as the *Life of Moses*.

23. **David Halperin (b. 1952)** is an American theorist of gender and sexuality and, at the time of writing, W. H. Auden Distinguished University Professor of the History and Theory of Sexuality at the University of Michigan. He has worked extensively on ancient and modern theories of sexuality and gender, focusing especially on Plato's erotic theory.

24. **Martin Heidegger (1889–1976)** was a German philosopher who has had a significant influence on contemporary philosophy. He is best known for his early work *Being and Time*.

25. **Heraclitus of Ephesus (circa 535–475 b.c.e.)** was a philosopher notable for his theory that all things are in a state of flux. Although none of his works survive, we know that he was the author of *On Nature*—a generic title used by many of the early philosophers covering cosmology, physics, morality, and epistemology.

26. **Herodotus (484–425 b.c.e.)** was a Greek historian from Halicarnassus renowned

for his systematic approach to the subject of history. His major work, the *Histories*, details the war between Greece and Persia.

27. **Homer (circa eighth century b.c.e.)** was an ancient composer of epic poetry, of great importance to the ancient Greeks. He is best known as the author of *The Iliad* and *The Odyssey*, which have had a lasting effect on Western thought and culture.

28. **Saul Kripke (b. 1940)** is an American philosopher and, at the time of writing, Professor Emeritus at Princeton University. His work focuses on areas including mathematical logic, epistemology, and the philosophy of language. He is the author of *Naming and Necessity*.

29. **Jacques Lacan (1901–81)** was a French psychoanalyst who built upon the insights of Sigmund Freud. Lacan's work was published as a series of seminars; the collection Écrits also contains some key essays.

30. **Anders Nygren (1890–1978)** was a Swedish theologian of the Lutheran (Protestant) tradition. His most famous work, *Agape and Eros*, argues that Christian love is fundamentally different from Greek Eros.

31. **Origen of Alexandria (circa 185–253 c.e.)** was an influential early Christian theologian and philosopher. He made use of Platonic and Neoplatonic ideas in his thinking about God, in numerous sermons, commentaries, and works such as *On Prayer* and *On First Principles*.

32. **Parmenides of Elea (late sixth or early fifth century b.c.e.)** was a philosopher. His *On Nature* is a metaphysical work about the division between an intelligible and true world of being and the sensible and false world of becoming.

33. **Petronius (27–66 c.e.)** was a writer and courtier who lived during the Roman Empire. His *Satyricon* contains elements that parody the luxurious lifestyle enjoyed by the emperor Nero.

34. **Philo of Alexandria (20 b.c.e.–50 C.E c.e.)** was a Jewish philosopher living in Egypt. His philosophy, notably in his key work *On the Contemplative Life*, attempted to create a synthesis between the ideas of Greek and Jewish philosophy.

35. **Plotinus (204–70 c.e.)** was a Greek Neoplatonist philosopher. His idea of the three principles of the One, the Intellect and the Soul, as explored in *The Enneads*, had a strong influence on Christian and Renaissance thought.
36. **Plutarch (46–120 c.e.)** was a Greek historian, essayist and biographer from Boeotia. His work *The Amatorius* is influenced by Plato's *Symposium* and likewise takes Eros as its subject.
37. **Hilary Putnam (1926–2016)** is an American philosopher in the analytic tradition. The author of works such as *Philosophy of Logic*, he specializes in mathematics, computer science, and the philosophy of mind.
38. **Peter Paul Rubens (1577–1640)** was a Flemish painter who lived in Antwerp, whose works are typical of the baroque style. He once painted a scene from Plato's *Symposium*.
39. **Bertrand Russell (1872–1970)** was a British analytic philosopher, noted for his activities as a mathematician, historian, and social critic. His most famous work is *Principia Mathematica*, which attempted to systematise mathematical study along the lines of logic.
40. **Percy Bysshe Shelley (1792–1822)** was an influential English Romantic poet. His work includes the classic poems *Ozymandias*, *Alastor* and *Prometheus Unbound*. He also translated Plato's *Symposium*.
41. **Socrates (469–399 b.c.e.)**, Plato's primary teacher, was an Athenian philosopher who features in *Symposium* and other of Plato's dialogues. He left behind no writings of his own. He was sentenced to death on charges of corrupting the youth of Athens and impiety.
42. **Solon (638–558 b.c.e.)** was a poet, lawmaker and politician in Athens. He introduced legislation designed to address the moral and political problems of the Athenian city-state in the late sixth century, and was revered as one of the seven sages of the ancient world.
43. **Theognis of Megara (circa sixth century b.c.e.)** was an ancient Greek lyric poet. All his surviving poetry is set at aristocratic symposia and conveys a wide range of practical, political, and moral advice.

44. **Gregory Vlastos (1907–91)** was a scholar of Plato and ancient philosophy. In his *The Philosophy of Socrates*, Vlastos defends the notion that a distinctively Socratic philosophy can be distinguished from that of Plato himself.
45. **Xenophon of Athens (430–354 b.c.e.)** was a philosopher and historian of the Greek and Persian empires. He wrote about Socrates and investigated questions of morality, political life, and household management.
46. **Zeno of Citium (334–262 b.c.e.)** was an ancient Greek philosopher who established the Stoic school of philosophy in Athens.

WORKS CITED

1. Aristotle. *The Nicomachean Ethics.* Translated by David Ross. Oxford: Oxford University Press, 1980.

2. Balaguer, Mark. "Platonism in Metaphysics." *Stanford Encyclopedia of Philosophy* Spring 2014 edition, edited by Edward N. Zalta. Accessed April 1, 2015, http://plato.stanford.edu/archives/spr2014/entries/platonism.

3. Barthes, Roland. *A Lover's Discourse: Fragments.* Translated by Richard Howard. London: Vintage, 2002.

4. Bell, Shannon. "Tomb of the Sacred Prostitute: *The Symposium.*" In *Shadow of Spirit: Postmodernism and Religion,* edited by Phillipa Berry and Andrew Wernick, 198–210. London: Routledge, 1992.

5. Benedict XVI. *Deus Caritas Est.* Encyclical letter on Christian love. December 25, 2005.

6. Berg, Steven. *Eros and the Intoxications of Enlightenment: On Plato's Symposium.* Albany, NY: State University of New York Press, 2010.

7. Bowery, Anne-Marie. "Diotima Tells Socrates a Story: A Narrative Analysis of Plato's *Symposium.*" In *Feminism and Ancient Philosophy*, edited by Julie K. Ward, 175–94. London: Routledge, 1996.

8. Brady, Bernard V. *Christian Love.* Washington DC: Georgetown University Press, 2003.

9. Carnes, Jeffrey. "The Myth Which is Not One: Construction of Discourse in Plato's Symposium." In *Rethinking Sexuality: Foucault and Classical Antiquity*, edited by David H. J. Larmour, Paul Allen Miller, and Charles Platter, 104–21. Princeton, NJ: Princeton University Press, 1998.

10. Collette-Ducic, Bernard. "Making Friends: The Stoic Conception of Love and Its Platonic Background." In *Ancient and Medieval Concepts of Friendship*, edited by Suzanne Stern-Gillet and Gary M. Gurtler SJ, 87–116. Albany, NY: State University of New York Press, 2014.

11. Corrigan, Kevin and Elena Glazov-Corrigan. *Plato's Dialectic at Play: Argument, Structure, and Myth in the Symposium.* University Park, PA: Pennsylvania State University Press, 2004.

12. Dover, K. "The Date of Plato's *Symposium.*" *Phronesis* 10 (1965): 2–20.
13. Eisner, Robert. *The Road to Daulis: Psychoanalysis, Psychology and Classical Mythology.* Syracuse, NY: Syracuse University Press, 1987.
14. Ficino, Marsilio. *Commentary on Plato's 'Symposium' on Love.* Translated by Sears Jayne. Dallas, TX: Spring Publications, 1985.
15. Forster, E. M. *Maurice: A Novel.* London: Penguin, 2005.
16. Foucault, Michel. *The Use of Pleasure.* Vol. 2 of *The History of Sexuality.* Translated by Robert Hurley. New York: Random House, 1990.
17. Freud, Sigmund. *Beyond the Pleasure Principle.* Translated by James Strachey. London and New York: W. W. Norton, 1961.
18. Guthrie, W. K. C. *A History of Greek Philosophy.* Vol. 4, *Plato: The Man and His Dialogues: Earlier Period.* Cambridge: Cambridge University Press, 1986.
19. Hadot, Pierre. *Philosophy as a Way of Life: Spiritual Exercises From Socrates to Foucault.* Translated by Michael Chase. Oxford: Wiley-Blackwell, 1995.
20. Halperin, David. *One Hundred Years of Homosexuality: and Other Essays on Greek Love.* London: Routledge, 1990.
21. "Plato and the Erotics of Narrativity." In *Innovations of Antiquity,* edited by Daniel Selden and Ralph Hexter, 95–126. New York, NY: Routledge, 1992.
22. Hunter, Richard. *Plato's Symposium.* Oxford: Oxford University Press, 2004.
23. Hyland, Drew. *Questioning Platonism: Continental Interpretations of Plato.* Albany, NY: State University of New York Press, 2004.
24. Kraut, Richard. Introduction to *The Blackwell Guide to Aristotle's Nicomachean Ethics*, edited by Richard Kraut. Oxford: Blackwell, 2006.
25. Kraye, Jill. "The Transformation of Platonic Love in the Italian Renaissance." In *Plato and the English Imagination,* edited by Anna Baldwin and Sarah Hutton, 76–85. Cambridge: Cambridge University Press, 1994.
26. Lacan, Jacques. *Écrits: The First Complete Edition in English.* Translated by Bruce Fink. New York and London: W. W. Norton, 2006.

27. Lear, Andrew. "Ancient Pederasty: An Introduction." In *A Companion to Greek and Roman Sexualities*, edited by Thomas K. Hubbard, 102–27. Chichester: Blackwell, 2014.

28. Luchesi, Michele A. "Love Theory and Political Practice in Plutarch." In *Eros in Ancient Greece*, edited by Ed Sanders, Chiara Thumiger, Chris Carey and Nick J. Lowe, 209–28. Oxford: Oxford University Press, 2013.

29. McCoy, Marina. *Plato on the Rhetoric of Philosophers and Sophists.* Cambridge: Cambridge University Press, 2011.

30. McGrath, Elizabeth. "'The Drunken Acibiades': Rubens's Picture of Plato's Symposium." *Journal of the Warburg and Courtauld Institutes* 46 (1983): 228–35.

31. Miller, Paul Allen. "The Classical Roots of Poststructuralism: Lacan, Derrida, and Foucault." *International Journal of the Classical Tradition* 5 (1998): 204–25.

32. Nails, Debra. *The People of Plato: A Prosopography of Plato and other Socratics.* Indianapolis: Hackett Publishing, 2002.

33. Nussbaum, Martha. "Platonic Love and Colorado Law: the Relevance of Ancient Greek Norms to Modern Sexual Controversies." *Virginia Law Review* 80 (1994): 1515–651.

34. Nygren, Anders. *Agape and Eros*. Translated by Philip Watson. London: SPCK, 1983.

35. Osborne, Catherine. *Eros Unveiled: Plato and the God of Love.* Oxford: Oxford University Press, 2002.

36. Philo of Alexandria. *The Contemplative Life, Giants and Selections.* Translated by David Winston. Mahwah, NJ: Paulist Press, 1981.

37. Pickstock, Catherine. "The Problem of Reported Speech: Friendship and Philosophy in Plato's *Lysis* and *Symposium.*" *New Blackfriars* 82 (2001): 525–40.

38. Plato. *Phaedrus.* Translated by Walter Hamilton. London: Penguin, 1973.

39. —— *The Symposium*. In Plato: The Symposium, translated by M. C. Howatson, edited by M. C. Howatson and Frisbee C. C. Sheffield. Cambridge: Cambridge University Press, 2008.

40. Plotinus. "Love." In *The Enneads*, translated by Stephen MacKenna, 174–86. London: Penguin Classics, 1991.
41. Price, A. W. *Love and Friendship in Plato and Aristotle*. Oxford: Oxford University Press, 1989.
42. Prior, William. "Developmentalism." In *The Continuum Companion to Plato*, edited by Gerald A. Press, 288–9. London: Continuum, 2012.
43. "Socrates (historical)." In *The Continuum Companion to Plato*, edited by Gerald A. Press, 28–30. London: Continuum, 2012.
44. Scott, Gary Alan and William A. Welton. *Erotic Wisdom: Philosophy and Intermediacy in Plato's Symposium*. Albany, NY: State University of New York Press, 2008.
45. Sheffield, Frisbee C. C. "Introduction." In Ploto: The Symposium, translated by M. C. Howatson, edited by M. C. Howatson and Frisbee C. C. Sheffield. Cambridge: Cambridge University Press, 2008.
46. *Plato's Symposium: The Ethics of Desire*. Oxford: Oxford University Press, 2006. Steiner, Deborah Tarn. *Images in Mind: Statues in Archaic and Classical Greek Literature and Thought*. Princeton, NJ: Princeton University Press, 2002.
47. Vlastos. Gregory. "The Individual as an Object of Love in Plato." In *Platonic Studies*, edited by Gregory Vlastos, 3–42. Princeton NJ: Princeton University Press, 1973.
48. Whitehead, A. N. *Process and Reality: An Essay in Cosmology*, corrected edition. New York: The Free Press, 1978.
49. Xenophon. *Conversations of Socrates*. Translated by Hugh Tredennick and Robin Waterfield. London: Penguin, 1990.
50. Zuckert, Catherine H. *Plato's Philosophers: The Coherence of the Dialogues*. Chicago: University of Chicago Press, 2009.

原书作者简介

柏拉图于公元前429年左右出生于雅典——古典时期的知识文化中心。柏拉图被认为是西方政治哲学、形而上学和伦理学传统中最具影响力的哲学家,他曾师从哲学家苏格拉底,并且担任哲学家亚里士多德的老师。他还建立了著名的"柏拉图学园"——雅典城郊一个重要的学习中心。柏拉图于公元前347年去世。

本书作者简介

理查德·埃利斯博士是加州大学洛杉矶分校古典文学系的讲师。他的研究兴趣包括古希腊哲学的各个领域,专攻前苏格拉底哲学、早期古希腊哲学和文学的交互,以及17世纪英国作家约翰·洛克的哲学。

西蒙·雷文斯克罗夫特博士是剑桥大学冯·许格尔天主教研究所的研究员。他的研究兴趣集中于神学、哲学、文学和政治及社会理论间的交互。他的博士论文研究激进社会理论家伊凡·伊里奇社会理论的哲学和神学基础。

世界名著中的批判性思维

《世界思想宝库钥匙丛书》致力于深入浅出地阐释全世界著名思想家的观点,不论是谁、在何处都能了解到,从而推进批判性思维发展。

《世界思想宝库钥匙丛书》与世界顶尖大学的一流学者合作,为一系列学科中最有影响的著作推出新的分析文本,介绍其观点和影响。在这一不断扩展的系列中,每种选入的著作都代表了历经时间考验的思想典范。通过为这些著作提供必要背景、揭示原作者的学术渊源以及说明这些著作所产生的影响,本系列图书希望让读者以新视角看待这些划时代的经典之作。读者应学会思考、运用并挑战这些著作中的观点,而不是简单接受它们。

ABOUT THE AUTHOR OF THE ORIGINAL WORK

Plato was born in Athens—then the intellectual center of the ancient world—around 429 b.c.e. Regarded as the most influential philosopher in the Western tradition of political philosophy, metaphysics, and ethics, Plato was a follower of the philosopher Socrates and teacher of the philosopher Aristotle. The founder of the famous Academy—an important center of learning just outside Athens—Plato died around 347 b.c.e.

ABOUT THE AUTHORS OF THE ANALYSIS

Dr Richard Ellis is a Lecturer in the Department of Classics at the University of California Los Angeles. His research interests include all areas of ancient Greek philosophy, with a specialisation in the Pre-Socratics, as well as the intersections between early Greek philosophy and literature and the philosophy of the 17th century British writer John Locke.

Dr Simon Ravenscroft is research fellow at theVon Hügel Institue for for Critical Catholic Enquiry at the University of Cambridge. His research interests sit at the intersection of theology, philosophy, literature, and political and social theory. His doctoral dissertation was on the philosophical and theological underpinnings of the social theory of the radical social theorist Ivan Illich.

ABOUT MACAT
GREAT WORKS FOR CRITICAL THINKING

Macat is focused on making the ideas of the world's great thinkers accessible and comprehensible to everybody, everywhere, in ways that promote the development of enhanced critical thinking skills.

It works with leading academics from the world's top universities to produce new analyses that focus on the ideas and the impact of the most influential works ever written across a wide variety of academic disciplines. Each of the works that sit at the heart of its growing library is an enduring example of great thinking. But by setting them in context — and looking at the influences that shaped their authors, as well as the responses they provoked — Macat encourages readers to look at these classics and game-changers with fresh eyes. Readers learn to think, engage and challenge their ideas, rather than simply accepting them.

批判性思维与《会饮篇》

首要批判性思维技巧：理性化思维

次要批判性思维技巧：评估

  柏拉图作于公元前 4 世纪早期的《会饮篇》，证实了理性化思维与评估的力量有多么的强大。

  《会饮篇》因其对爱与知识间关系的开创性论述而为人周知，它同时是一部经典文本，展现出可以界定柏拉图整个作品体系的批判性思维技巧。理性化思维是组织论据及有说服力地阐释自身观点的技巧；评估则与判断观点的说服力、相关性及其可接受性相关。柏拉图的哲学对话手法是这两种技巧完美结合的范式。柏拉图虚构了一场晚宴上的论辩，参加者是富有的雅典人，他们必须依次回应彼此的论点和观念，这意味着在每一个阶段，柏拉图都会对之前的观点进行评估，来判断其说服力及相关性，然后（通过下一个人）继续推理出一个新的观点来进行回应。

  柏拉图对哲学思维方式的影响是无与伦比的，他对于对话的运用就是这两种关键的批判性思维技巧的不二例证。

CRITICAL THINKING AND *SYMPOSIUM*

- Primary critical thinking skill: REASONING
- Secondary critical thinking skill: EVALUATION

Plato's *Symposium*, composed in the early fourth century BC, demonstrates just how powerful the skills of reasoning and evaluation can be.

Known to philosophers for its seminal discussion of the relationship of love to knowledge, *Symposium* is also a classic text that shows the critical thinking skills that define Plato's whole body of work in action. Reasoning is the skill of producing arguments and presenting a persuasive case for one's point of view; evaluation is about judging the strength of arguments, their relevance and their acceptability. Plato's philosophical technique of dialogue is the perfect frame for these two skills. Staging a fictional debate between characters (wealthy Athenians at a dinner party) who must respond in turn to each others' arguments and points of view means that, at every stage, Plato evaluates the previous argument, assesses its strength and relevance, and then proceeds (through the next character) to reason out a new argument in response.

Exerting unparalleled influence on the techniques of philosophical thought, Plato's use of dialogue is a supreme example of these two crucial critical thinking skills.

《世界思想宝库钥匙丛书》简介

《世界思想宝库钥匙丛书》致力于为一系列在各领域产生重大影响的人文社科类经典著作提供独特的学术探讨。每一本读物都不仅仅是原经典著作的内容摘要,而是介绍并深入研究原经典著作的学术渊源、主要观点和历史影响。这一丛书的目的是提供一套学习资料,以促进读者掌握批判性思维,从而更全面、深刻地去理解重要思想。

每一本读物分为 3 个部分:学术渊源、学术思想和学术影响,每个部分下有 4 个小节。这些章节旨在从各个方面研究原经典著作及其反响。

由于独特的体例,每一本读物不但易于阅读,而且另有一项优点:所有读物的编排体例相同,读者在进行某个知识层面的调查或研究时可交叉参阅多本该丛书中的相关读物,从而开启跨领域研究的路径。

为了方便阅读,每本读物最后还列出了术语表和人名表(在书中则以星号 * 标记),此外还有参考文献。

《世界思想宝库钥匙丛书》与剑桥大学合作,理清了批判性思维的要点,即如何通过 6 种技能来进行有效思考。其中 3 种技能让我们能够理解问题,另 3 种技能让我们有能力解决问题。这 6 种技能合称为"批判性思维 PACIER 模式",它们是:

分析:了解如何建立一个观点;
评估:研究一个观点的优点和缺点;
阐释:对意义所产生的问题加以理解;
创造性思维:提出新的见解,发现新的联系;
解决问题:提出切实有效的解决办法;
理性化思维:创建有说服力的观点。

THE MACAT LIBRARY

The Macat Library is a series of unique academic explorations of seminal works in the humanities and social sciences — books and papers that have had a significant and widely recognised impact on their disciplines. It has been created to serve as much more than just a summary of what lies between the covers of a great book. It illuminates and explores the influences on, ideas of, and impact of that book. Our goal is to offer a learning resource that encourages critical thinking and fosters a better, deeper understanding of important ideas.

Each publication is divided into three Sections: Influences, Ideas, and Impact. Each Section has four Modules. These explore every important facet of the work, and the responses to it.

This Section-Module structure makes a Macat Library book easy to use, but it has another important feature. Because each Macat book is written to the same format, it is possible (and encouraged!) to cross-reference multiple Macat books along the same lines of inquiry or research. This allows the reader to open up interesting interdisciplinary pathways.

To further aid your reading, lists of glossary terms and people mentioned are included at the end of this book (these are indicated by an asterisk [*] throughout) — as well as a list of works cited.

Macat has worked with the University of Cambridge to identify the elements of critical thinking and understand the ways in which six different skills combine to enable effective thinking.

Three allow us to fully understand a problem; three more give us the tools to solve it. Together, these six skills make up the PACIER model of critical thinking. They are:

ANALYSIS — understanding how an argument is built
EVALUATION — exploring the strengths and weaknesses of an argument
INTERPRETATION — understanding issues of meaning
CREATIVE THINKING — coming up with new ideas and fresh connections
PROBLEM-SOLVING — producing strong solutions
REASONING — creating strong arguments

"《世界思想宝库钥匙丛书》提供了独一无二的跨学科学习和研究工具。它介绍那些革新了各自学科研究的经典著作,还邀请全世界一流专家和教育机构进行严谨的分析,为每位读者打开世界顶级教育的大门。"

——安德烈亚斯·施莱歇尔,
经济合作与发展组织教育与技能司司长

"《世界思想宝库钥匙丛书》直面大学教育的巨大挑战……他们组建了一支精干而活跃的学者队伍,来推出在研究广度上颇具新意的教学材料。"

——布罗尔斯教授、勋爵,剑桥大学前校长

"《世界思想宝库钥匙丛书》的愿景令人赞叹。它通过分析和阐释那些曾深刻影响人类思想以及社会、经济发展的经典文本,提供了新的学习方法。它推动批判性思维,这对于任何社会和经济体来说都是至关重要的。这就是未来的学习方法。"

——查尔斯·克拉克阁下,英国前教育大臣

"对于那些影响了各自领域的著作,《世界思想宝库钥匙丛书》能让人们立即了解到围绕那些著作展开的评论性言论,这让该系列图书成为在这些领域从事研究的师生们不可或缺的资源。"

——威廉·特朗佐教授,加利福尼亚大学圣地亚哥分校

"Macat offers an amazing first-of-its-kind tool for interdisciplinary learning and research. Its focus on works that transformed their disciplines and its rigorous approach, drawing on the world's leading experts and educational institutions, opens up a world-class education to anyone."

—— Andreas Schleicher, Director for Education and Skills, Organisation for Economic Co-operation and Development

"Macat is taking on some of the major challenges in university education... They have drawn together a strong team of active academics who are producing teaching materials that are novel in the breadth of their approach."

—— Prof Lord Broers, former Vice-Chancellor of the University of Cambridge

"The Macat vision is exceptionally exciting. It focuses upon new modes of learning which analyse and explain seminal texts which have profoundly influenced world thinking and so social and economic development. It promotes the kind of critical thinking which is essential for any society and economy. This is the learning of the future."

—— Rt Hon Charles Clarke, former UK Secretary of State for Education

"The Macat analyses provide immediate access to the critical conversation surrounding the books that have shaped their respective discipline, which will make them an invaluable resource to all of those, students and teachers, working in the field."

—— Prof William Tronzo, University of California at San Diego

The Macat Library
世界思想宝库钥匙丛书

TITLE	中文书名	类别
An Analysis of Arjun Appadurai's *Modernity at Large: Cultural Dimensions of Globalization*	解析阿尔君·阿帕杜莱《消失的现代性：全球化的文化维度》	人类学
An Analysis of Claude Lévi-Strauss's *Structural Anthropology*	解析克劳德·列维-斯特劳斯《结构人类学》	人类学
An Analysis of Marcel Mauss's *The Gift*	解析马塞尔·莫斯《礼物》	人类学
An Analysis of Jared M. Diamond's *Guns, Germs, and Steel: The Fate of Human Societies*	解析贾雷德·M.戴蒙德《枪炮、病菌与钢铁：人类社会的命运》	人类学
An Analysis of Clifford Geertz's *The Interpretation of Cultures*	解析克利福德·格尔茨《文化的解释》	人类学
An Analysis of Philippe Ariès's *Centuries of Childhood: A Social History of Family Life*	解析菲力浦·阿利埃斯《儿童的世纪：旧制度下的儿童和家庭生活》	人类学
An Analysis of W. Chan Kim & Renée Mauborgne's *Blue Ocean Strategy*	解析金伟灿／勒妮·莫博涅《蓝海战略》	商业
An Analysis of John P. Kotter's *Leading Change*	解析约翰·P.科特《领导变革》	商业
An Analysis of Michael E. Porter's *Competitive Strategy: Techniques for Analyzing Industries and Competitors*	解析迈克尔·E.波特《竞争战略：分析产业和竞争对手的技术》	商业
An Analysis of Jean Lave & Etienne Wenger's *Situated Learning: Legitimate Peripheral Participation*	解析琼·莱夫／艾蒂纳·温格《情境学习：合法的边缘性参与》	商业
An Analysis of Douglas McGregor's *The Human Side of Enterprise*	解析道格拉斯·麦格雷戈《企业的人性面》	商业
An Analysis of Milton Friedman's *Capitalism and Freedom*	解析米尔顿·弗里德曼《资本主义与自由》	商业
An Analysis of Ludwig von Mises's *The Theory of Money and Credit*	解析路德维希·冯·米塞斯《货币和信用理论》	经济学
An Analysis of Adam Smith's *The Wealth of Nations*	解析亚当·斯密《国富论》	经济学
An Analysis of Thomas Piketty's *Capital in the Twenty-First Century*	解析托马斯·皮凯蒂《21世纪资本论》	经济学
An Analysis of Nassim Nicholas Taleb's *The Black Swan: The Impact of the Highly Improbable*	解析纳西姆·尼古拉斯·塔勒布《黑天鹅：如何应对不可预知的未来》	经济学
An Analysis of Ha-Joon Chang's *Kicking Away the Ladder*	解析张夏准《富国陷阱：发达国家为何踢开梯子》	经济学
An Analysis of Thomas Robert Malthus's *An Essay on the Principle of Population*	解析托马斯·罗伯特·马尔萨斯《人口论》	经济学

An Analysis of John Maynard Keynes's *The General Theory of Employment, Interest and Money*	解析约翰·梅纳德·凯恩斯《就业、利息和货币通论》	经济学
An Analysis of Milton Friedman's *The Role of Monetary Policy*	解析米尔顿·弗里德曼《货币政策的作用》	经济学
An Analysis of Burton G. Malkiel's *A Random Walk Down Wall Street*	解析伯顿·G.马尔基尔《漫步华尔街》	经济学
An Analysis of Friedrich A. Hayek's *The Road to Serfdom*	解析弗里德里希·A.哈耶克《通往奴役之路》	经济学
An Analysis of Charles P. Kindleberger's *Manias, Panics, and Crashes: A History of Financial Crises*	解析查尔斯·P.金德尔伯格《疯狂、惊恐和崩溃：金融危机史》	经济学
An Analysis of Amartya Sen's *Development as Freedom*	解析阿马蒂亚·森《以自由看待发展》	经济学
An Analysis of Rachel Carson's *Silent Spring*	解析蕾切尔·卡森《寂静的春天》	地理学
An Analysis of Charles Darwin's *On the Origin of Species: by Means of Natural Selection, or The Preservation of Favoured Races in the Struggle for Life*	解析查尔斯·达尔文《物种起源》	地理学
An Analysis of World Commission on Environment and Development's *The Brundtland Report: Our Common Future*	解析世界环境与发展委员会《布伦特兰报告：我们共同的未来》	地理学
An Analysis of James E. Lovelock's *Gaia: A New Look at Life on Earth*	解析詹姆斯·E.拉伍洛克《盖娅：地球生命的新视野》	地理学
An Analysis of Paul Kennedy's *The Rise and Fall of the Great Powers: Economic Change and Military Conflict from 1500–2000*	解析保罗·肯尼迪《大国的兴衰：1500—2000年的经济变革与军事冲突》	历史
An Analysis of Janet L. Abu-Lughod's *Before European Hegemony: The World System A. D. 1250–1350*	解析珍妮特·L.阿布-卢格霍德《欧洲霸权之前：1250—1350年的世界体系》	历史
An Analysis of Alfred W. Crosby's *The Columbian Exchange: Biological and Cultural Consequences of 1492*	解析艾尔弗雷德·W.克罗斯比《哥伦布大交换：1492年以后的生物影响和文化冲击》	历史
An Analysis of Tony Judt's *Postwar: A History of Europe since 1945*	解析托尼·朱特《战后欧洲史》	历史
An Analysis of Richard J. Evans's *In Defence of History*	解析理查德·J.艾文斯《捍卫历史》	历史
An Analysis of Eric Hobsbawm's *The Age of Revolution: Europe 1789–1848*	解析艾瑞克·霍布斯鲍姆《革命的年代：欧洲1789—1848年》	历史

An Analysis of Roland Barthes's *Mythologies*	解析罗兰·巴特《神话学》	文学与批判理论
An Analysis of Simone de Beauvoir's *The Second Sex*	解析西蒙娜·德·波伏娃《第二性》	文学与批判理论
An Analysis of Edward W. Said's *Orientalism*	解析爱德华·W. 萨义德《东方主义》	文学与批判理论
An Analysis of Virginia Woolf's *A Room of One's Own*	解析弗吉尼亚·伍尔芙《一间自己的房间》	文学与批判理论
An Analysis of Judith Butler's *Gender Trouble*	解析朱迪斯·巴特勒《性别麻烦》	文学与批判理论
An Analysis of Ferdinand de Saussure's *Course in General Linguistics*	解析费尔迪南·德·索绪尔《普通语言学教程》	文学与批判理论
An Analysis of Susan Sontag's *On Photography*	解析苏珊·桑塔格《论摄影》	文学与批判理论
An Analysis of Walter Benjamin's *The Work of Art in the Age of Mechanical Reproduction*	解析瓦尔特·本雅明《机械复制时代的艺术作品》	文学与批判理论
An Analysis of W. E. B. Du Bois's *The Souls of Black Folk*	解析W.E.B. 杜波依斯《黑人的灵魂》	文学与批判理论
An Analysis of Plato's *The Republic*	解析柏拉图《理想国》	哲学
An Analysis of Plato's *Symposium*	解析柏拉图《会饮篇》	哲学
An Analysis of Aristotle's *Metaphysics*	解析亚里士多德《形而上学》	哲学
An Analysis of Aristotle's *Nicomachean Ethics*	解析亚里士多德《尼各马可伦理学》	哲学
An Analysis of Immanuel Kant's *Critique of Pure Reason*	解析伊曼努尔·康德《纯粹理性批判》	哲学
An Analysis of Ludwig Wittgenstein's *Philosophical Investigations*	解析路德维希·维特根斯坦《哲学研究》	哲学
An Analysis of G. W. F. Hegel's *Phenomenology of Spirit*	解析G. W. F. 黑格尔《精神现象学》	哲学
An Analysis of Baruch Spinoza's *Ethics*	解析巴鲁赫·斯宾诺莎《伦理学》	哲学
An Analysis of Hannah Arendt's *The Human Condition*	解析汉娜·阿伦特《人的境况》	哲学
An Analysis of G. E. M. Anscombe's *Modern Moral Philosophy*	解析G. E. M. 安斯康姆《现代道德哲学》	哲学
An Analysis of David Hume's *An Enquiry Concerning Human Understanding*	解析大卫·休谟《人类理解研究》	哲学

An Analysis of Søren Kierkegaard's *Fear and Trembling*	解析索伦·克尔凯郭尔《恐惧与战栗》	哲学
An Analysis of René Descartes's *Meditations on First Philosophy*	解析勒内·笛卡尔《第一哲学沉思录》	哲学
An Analysis of Friedrich Nietzsche's *On the Genealogy of Morality*	解析弗里德里希·尼采《论道德的谱系》	哲学
An Analysis of Gilbert Ryle's *The Concept of Mind*	解析吉尔伯特·赖尔《心的概念》	哲学
An Analysis of Thomas Kuhn's *The Structure of Scientific Revolutions*	解析托马斯·库恩《科学革命的结构》	哲学
An Analysis of John Stuart Mill's *Utilitarianism*	解析约翰·斯图亚特·穆勒《功利主义》	哲学
An Analysis of Aristotle's *Politics*	解析亚里士多德《政治学》	政治学
An Analysis of Niccolò Machiavelli's *The Prince*	解析尼科洛·马基雅维利《君主论》	政治学
An Analysis of Karl Marx's *Capital*	解析卡尔·马克思《资本论》	政治学
An Analysis of Benedict Anderson's *Imagined Communities*	解析本尼迪克特·安德森《想象的共同体》	政治学
An Analysis of Samuel P. Huntington's *The Clash of Civilizations and the Remaking of World Order*	解析塞缪尔·P.亨廷顿《文明的冲突与世界秩序的重建》	政治学
An Analysis of Alexis de Tocqueville's *Democracy in America*	解析阿列克西·德·托克维尔《论美国的民主》	政治学
An Analysis of John A. Hobson's *Imperialism: A Study*	解析约翰·A.霍布森《帝国主义》	政治学
An Analysis of Thomas Paine's *Common Sense*	解析托马斯·潘恩《常识》	政治学
An Analysis of John Rawls's *A Theory of Justice*	解析约翰·罗尔斯《正义论》	政治学
An Analysis of Francis Fukuyama's *The End of History and the Last Man*	解析弗朗西斯·福山《历史的终结与最后的人》	政治学
An Analysis of John Locke's *Two Treatises of Government*	解析约翰·洛克《政府论》	政治学
An Analysis of Sun Tzu's *The Art of War*	解析孙武《孙子兵法》	政治学
An Analysis of Henry Kissinger's *World Order: Reflections on the Character of Nations and the Course of History*	解析亨利·基辛格《世界秩序》	政治学
An Analysis of Jean-Jacques Rousseau's *The Social Contract*	解析让-雅克·卢梭《社会契约论》	政治学

An Analysis of Odd Arne Westad's *The Global Cold War: Third World Interventions and the Making of Our Times*	解析文安立《全球冷战：美苏对第三世界的干涉与当代世界的形成》	政治学
An Analysis of Sigmund Freud's *The Interpretation of Dreams*	解析西格蒙德·弗洛伊德《梦的解析》	心理学
An Analysis of William James' *The Principles of Psychology*	解析威廉·詹姆斯《心理学原理》	心理学
An Analysis of Philip Zimbardo's *The Lucifer Effect*	解析菲利普·津巴多《路西法效应》	心理学
An Analysis of Leon Festinger's *A Theory of Cognitive Dissonance*	解析利昂·费斯汀格《认知失调论》	心理学
An Analysis of Richard H. Thaler & Cass R. Sunstein's *Nudge: Improving Decisions about Health, Wealth, and Happiness*	解析理查德·H. 泰勒／卡斯·R. 桑斯坦《助推：如何做出有关健康、财富和幸福的更优决策》	心理学
An Analysis of Gordon Allport's *The Nature of Prejudice*	解析高尔登·奥尔波特《偏见的本质》	心理学
An Analysis of Steven Pinker's *The Better Angels of Our Nature: Why Violence Has Declined*	解析斯蒂芬·平克《人性中的善良天使：暴力为什么会减少》	心理学
An Analysis of Stanley Milgram's *Obedience to Authority*	解析斯坦利·米尔格拉姆《对权威的服从》	心理学
An Analysis of Betty Friedan's *The Feminine Mystique*	解析贝蒂·弗里丹《女性的奥秘》	心理学
An Analysis of David Riesman's *The Lonely Crowd: A Study of the Changing American Character*	解析大卫·理斯曼《孤独的人群：美国人社会性格演变之研究》	社会学
An Analysis of Franz Boas's *Race, Language and Culture*	解析弗朗兹·博厄斯《种族、语言与文化》	社会学
An Analysis of Pierre Bourdieu's *Outline of a Theory of Practice*	解析皮埃尔·布尔迪厄《实践理论大纲》	社会学
An Analysis of Max Weber's *The Protestant Ethic and the Spirit of Capitalism*	解析马克斯·韦伯《新教伦理与资本主义精神》	社会学
An Analysis of Jane Jacobs's *The Death and Life of Great American Cities*	解析简·雅各布斯《美国大城市的死与生》	社会学
An Analysis of C. Wright Mills's *The Sociological Imagination*	解析C. 赖特·米尔斯《社会学的想象力》	社会学
An Analysis of Robert E. Lucas Jr.'s *Why Doesn't Capital Flow from Rich to Poor Countries?*	解析小罗伯特·E. 卢卡斯《为何资本不从富国流向穷国？》	社会学

An Analysis of Émile Durkheim's *On Suicide*	解析埃米尔·迪尔凯姆《自杀论》	社会学
An Analysis of Eric Hoffer's *The True Believer: Thoughts on the Nature of Mass Movements*	解析埃里克·霍弗《狂热分子：群众运动圣经》	社会学
An Analysis of Jared M. Diamond's *Collapse: How Societies Choose to Fail or Survive*	解析贾雷德·M.戴蒙德《大崩溃：社会如何选择兴亡》	社会学
An Analysis of Michel Foucault's *The History of Sexuality Vol. 1: The Will to Knowledge*	解析米歇尔·福柯《性史（第一卷）：求知意志》	社会学
An Analysis of Michel Foucault's *Discipline and Punish*	解析米歇尔·福柯《规训与惩罚》	社会学
An Analysis of Richard Dawkins's *The Selfish Gene*	解析理查德·道金斯《自私的基因》	社会学
An Analysis of Antonio Gramsci's *Prison Notebooks*	解析安东尼奥·葛兰西《狱中札记》	社会学
An Analysis of Augustine's *Confessions*	解析奥古斯丁《忏悔录》	神学
An Analysis of C. S. Lewis's *The Abolition of Man*	解析 C. S. 路易斯《人之废》	神学

图书在版编目（CIP）数据

解析柏拉图《会饮篇》：汉、英 / 理查德·埃利斯（Richard Ellis），西蒙·雷文斯克罗夫特（Simon Ravenscroft）著；李梦千译. —上海：上海外语教育出版社，2021
（世界思想宝库钥匙丛书）
ISBN 978-7-5446-6670-1

Ⅰ.①解… Ⅱ.①理… ②赛… ③李… Ⅲ.①柏拉图（Plato 前427–前347）－哲学思想－汉、英 Ⅳ.①B502.232

中国版本图书馆CIP数据核字（2021）第028801号

This Chinese-English bilingual edition of *An Analysis of Plato's Symposium* is published by arrangement with Macat International Limited.
Licensed for sale throughout the world.

本书汉英双语版由Macat国际有限公司授权上海外语教育出版社有限公司出版。
供在全世界范围内发行、销售。

图字：09 – 2018 – 549

出版发行：**上海外语教育出版社**
　　　　　（上海外国语大学内）　邮编：200083
电　　话：021-65425300（总机）
电子邮箱：bookinfo@sflep.com.cn
网　　址：http://www.sflep.com
责任编辑：李振荣

印　　刷：上海信老印刷厂
开　　本：890×1240　1/32　印张 6　字数 123千字
版　　次：2021年8月第1版　2021年8月第1次印刷
书　　号：ISBN 978-7-5446-6670-1
定　　价：30.00 元
本版图书如有印装质量问题，可向本社调换
质量服务热线：4008-213-263　电子邮箱：editorial@sflep.com